THE 19th HOLE

❛ You're only here for a short visit.
Don't hurry, don't worry, and be sure
to smell the flowers along the way. ❜

WALTER HAGEN

First published in Great Britain in 1996 by

Chameleon Books

106 Great Russell Street

London WC1B 3LJ

Copyright for text © DC Publications Ltd

All rights reserved

CIP data for this title is available from the British Library

ISBN 0 233 99052 6

Book and jacket design by Jupiter 7 Graphics Ltd

Printed in Spain by Graficas Zamudio Printek, S.A.L.

ACKNOWLEDGEMENTS:
Special thanks to Gaynor Edwards,
Mary Killingworth, Mark Peacock, Gail Ashton,
Paula O'Brien, Edwin Donald, Tim Hawkins,
Angus Miller, all at Generation Associates,
all the keen golfers across the country who
kindly supplied us with their stories, Stephanie
Goodwin and the man who made it all possible
- Tim Forrester.

A special thanks to Adrian Murrell and all the
lads at Allsport Picture Agency.

Dedicated to The Endangered Species Golf Society
The Greys Green Golf Club, Peppard
of which I am a founder member
David Crowe

Nigel Bond, Les Clarke, Jim Davis, Gary Edmonds, Charles Hoatson,
Jack Lunnon, Steve Lynas, John Vaughan, Ken Vaughan,
Mike Windsor and Keith Wyness

To Joe Crowe who cut the grass and Alexander Hood who owns it

For me, like any golfer, the friends and good times that go with golf are just as important as the playing itself. Whether you're cracking the champagne after a Tour victory or enjoying a beer and a joke with your pals after a social four ball, there's always something about golf that can put a smile on your face.

This collection of golf stories, quotes and pictures shows the fun side of golf. It's called The 19th Hole and I hope you enjoy it as much as the first 18.

Bernard Gallacher

Bernard Gallacher, OBE

Bernard Gallacher's writer's fee for this publication was donated to The Golf Foundation, a registered charity, at his request.

OUT OF AFRICA

DURING A RECENT visit to South Africa, my son-in-law and I arranged a round at a Northern Transvaal course which bordered onto the Kruger National Park. We were met in the car park by several would-be-caddies. We selected two guides from the assembled throng. Mine had a bad limp, while the one now accompanying my son-in-law had the physique of a stick insect with anorexia. With the officials' instructions to watch our property, drink plenty of water and be wary of any missing or damaged boundary fences firmly in mind, we set off on our round. To indicate how hot it was that day I momentarily rested my wedge on the bridge of my foot, yanking it away almost instantly but not before I had branded across my right hoof the word 'Slazenger'.

It was as we were making our way down the par 5 seventh, which runs parallel to the game reserve, that we were transfixed to the spot by a lion's roar. With a dry throat I croaked, "Take out an iron son, and quietly change your golf shoes for your trainers". My son-in-law looked at me as though I had been struck with mad cow disease and without moving his lips hissed, "We will never outrun a lion Dad."

"We won't have to," I whispered. "We just have to outrun these two," indicating our well-worn caddies. Needless to say we moved sideways faster than a shanked 4 iron and played the last couple of holes without further incident.

MR R SANDS (CLEETHORPES)

A LONG HOLE

TWO JAPANESE GOLFERS playing the local golf course for the first time, and possibly playing golf for the first time, teed off the first ahead of me. I watched the tee shots land near the marker post at the first. Although accurate, they still had a fairly long second shot to the green. I watched as they took the marker post out, in case they hit it with the second shots. To my amazement they proceeded to putt out into the post hole. I had to laugh as one of them rolled up his sleeve trying to get his ball out of the long deep post hole.

MR G WOOD (LIVINGSTON)

WHEN I WAS IN INDIA

WHILST SERVING in 238 Squadron RAF in India during the war we were in transit to Australia and domiciled in a transit camp in Calcutta. Four of us decided to go to the Royal Calcutta golf club at Tolleygunge for a game. Clubs, balls and caddies were all provided by the members of the club for use of service personnel. We duly set off on number one and on reaching the green my small Indian caddie gave me a putter. I had the shock of my life for stamped on the head of the putter was GV Tuck, Bridlington Golf Club; my father, who was a professional golfer. He must have made it whilst he was a pro at that club around 1910. I asked if I could purchase the putter but was refused. Upon returning for another game later I was given the club, which I still have to this day.

MR R TUCK (STAFFORD)

Golf For beginners. Lesson 1: addressing the ball.

OFF TO A BAD START

THE PLEASINGTON GOLF CLUB near where I live is a rather exclusive club with an eight year waiting list. My friend, Alec, who had patiently waited these eight years, finally received notice that his membership had come through.

Being the eager type, he decided to have a game the very first day of his new membership and was about to play his shot from just in front of the yellow tee on the first hole when a chap approached him and said "Excuse me, are you a member?" Alec, indignant at the rude interruption said "I am as a matter of fact, I just joined today and this is my first round." "Well, don't you know the rules? You're supposed to tee off from behind the yellow tees," the stranger said. "Who are you?" said Alec. "I just happen to be the President," was the snobbish reply from the man. "Well, will you piss off and let me play my second shot?" said Alec.

MR N McKILLOP-SMITH (BLACKBURN, LANCS)

NONE HIT WONDER

A MAN WENT INTO his local golf Pro shop and asked to purchase the best set of clubs in the shop because he was going to start playing golf. The Pro showed him the best clubs in the shop and told the man they were £1,000. "I'll take them," said the man "and the golf ball as well." The Pro replied "You can have a golf ball for nothing, but will one be enough?" "Yes," said the man, "that will do fine" and off he went with the clubs and the ball.

Six months later the man returned to the shop and said to the Pro, "Can I have another set of clubs as I've worn the others out?" The Pro replied, "You can't have done, let me see them." On inspection the Pro said "You're quite right, they are worn out, you must have played a lot of golf, I have never seen a set of clubs wear out as quickly as these. Unfortunately a new set will cost £1,000." "That's OK" said the man. The Pro then asked the man if he required some more balls, to which the man replied, "No thanks, I haven't managed to hit the last one yet!"

MR M LORD (HASTINGS, E SUSSEX)

TROUBLESHOOTING

THERE WERE TWO golfers on the first tee. Bill went first and hit his drive 20 ft in front of him. Then turned to his partner and said "I know what went wrong, I was standing too close to the ball." His partner replied, "You're not standing far from it now."

MR H MORL (CHESTER)

> **'This game is great and very strange.'**
>
> SEVE BALLESTEROS

BIG HITTER

A MAN TOOK his monkey to the golf club and challenged the club professional to a round of golf for £100 a side with the monkey. The club professional accepted, thinking there was no way he could lose to a monkey. They went to the first tee, a 550 yards par 5. The monkey went first, driving the ball 550 yards and finishing about six inches from the hole. On seeing this the club professional had second thoughts, called the game off and paid the monkey's owner £100. As an afterthought the club professional asked the owner of the monkey what his pet's putting was like. The monkey's owner replied, same as his driving, 550 yards.

MR K GRANT (LEEDS)

> **6 If the golfer's object was merely to sink the ball in the hole, he could walk around the course with a bag of golf balls and drop each one in. 9**
>
> ARNOLD LUNN

A SLOW BACK SWING

OUR LADY CAPTAIN was playing a round of golf with three other members including a senior male member, noted for his dry humour. In front was a young man with a full complement of new golf clubs plus every available aide to golfers imaginable. The young man's game was decidedly slow, he swung and missed the ball time and again. Finally he turned and apologised whereupon our senior player in his broadest Yorkshire accent said "Nay lad! we don't mind tha' missing the ball, but can tha' miss it a bit faster." Needless to say, nobody played very good golf after that.

MRS J CUDDY (LEEDS)

LAST MINUTE HERO

THIS STORY RELATES to a better ball stapleford competition, which turned out to be a very bitter-sweet affair for my partner. I was, and am, a genuine 28 handicap golfer. My partner (selected by a draw) was a 19 handicap. The scene was Crook golf club in County Durham. Even by my own standards this day was turning out to be a disaster. On the front nine, I only experienced 5 greens, losing 6 balls in the process. By halfway my partner's score had counted on all nine holes and as a team we had a respectable total.

My trail of disaster continued with more lost balls and lack of putting practice, while my partner continued to grind away consistently with bogies and pars. By the completion of the seventeenth hole my partner's score had counted on every hole with only one "one pointer", many "two pointers" and enough "three pointers" to give optimism of a respectable finish without my input. On the par 4 eighteenth, my partner drove off with his usual boring 190 yard-ish drive. Now every golfer will know how I felt at that time; nothing had gone right all day, partner is in a good position, nothing to lose, what the hell!

Yes, best drive of the day 2 yards behind my partner, a massive drive for me. Second shot in same frame of mind, best 4 iron of the day for me, stops on front edge of bunker situated about 4 yards in front of the green. Partner misclubs slightly and finishes slightly behind me. True to form my partner plays his third shot on to the very difficult sloping green and leaves the ball stone dead.

Now to appreciate fully the climax to this round, it is important to note that in addition to having a very serious right to left slope, the eighteenth green is very close to the clubhouse which has a very large window area overlooking the green. Our foursome was the last one out on the course. All other pairings scores were therefore already posted and a large audience awaited the conclusion. With another 3 points from my partner already in the bag, I was under no pressure when I played a quite respectable chip from the edge of the bunker onto the green about 15 feet to the right of the pin. Rolling faster than I would have liked, the ball turned down the green, its passage to the rough at the bottom of the green was only stopped by the pin and then the hole! - 4 points!

My instant reaction was relief that at last I had contributed something to the team's score. However, on entering the clubhouse and announcing our respectable score, it transpired that we had won the competition by one point and as far as the "gallery" was concerned I was the star. My partner, having played one of his best rounds ever, probably felt like throwing his clubs into the nearest water hazard and I on the basis of one shot, had the most successful day of my career.

MR A OSBORNE (STOCKTON-ON-TEES)

WELL AND TRULY SNOOKERED

WHILST PLAYING the 12th hole at Belhus Park Golf Course last summer, my second shot to the green was over 200 yards so I decided to take a 3 wood to get as close as possible. As I hit the ball it flew straight for the green, landed 60 yards away and just kept going along the scorched hard ground.

There was one person on the green about to putt his ball 10 ft to the hole. My partner and I shouted 'fore' but he could not hear us.

My ball flew along the ground, up the sloped green, hit the other player's ball as he went to strike it with his putter. Talk about laugh, the fellow on the green looked like Norman Wisdom playing golf as he wobbled about not knowing where his ball had gone as it happened so fast, like a snooker shot!

It was a long walk to apologise.

MR S E GRAY (ESSEX)

ALWAYS CARRY A SPARE

I WAS TALKING to my local pro (now deceased) and he told me of a game he played with a fellow pro. It was a game with a large side stake and it was all square with one hole to play. My pro hit one down the middle, whilst the other pro hooked into the woods. My fellow got to the woods first and found the ball. He picked it up and put it in his pocket and carried on 'looking'. The other pro was some way away when he said it's OK I've found it. My pro said, he couldn't call him a cheat because he had his opponent's ball in his pocket.

The other pro had not only dropped another ball but it was a perfect line to the green. The match was halved, but the irony was if my fellow had left the ball he would have won because his opponent could only chip out.

MR A M SKILLEN (CHESHIRE)

ONE IN THE HAND IS WORTH THREE IN THE BUSH

WHILST PLAYING a so called 4 ball friendly at Mannings Heath, Sussex, my partner, playing last, stood on the tee and hit his ball off the toe of the club, straight into dense bushes which were about ten feet away. He walked slowly to the bag, took out a new ball from a pack of three and placed it on the tee. He did exactly the same again, resulting in the loss of another ball. He solemnly and without saying a word took another new ball out of the pack, examined it close to his face and then threw it into the hedge saying, "There you are, that's where you want to go isn't it." The rest of us fell about laughing. It certainly broke the tension.

MR O'SHEA (SURREY)

LOST BALL

LOCAL RULE ON a Liverpool municipal golf course: "Ball is not deemed to be lost until it has stopped rolling."

ALL MOD CONS

A YOUNG APPRENTICE mechanic on his first day at work at the Rolls Royce garage. The boss approaches him and asks him if he will clean a Rolls Royce Silver Shadow out, which belongs to a professional golfer. Whilst the apprentice is cleaning the car out he comes across a few golf tees on the floor of the car. Two hours later when the lad had finished cleaning the car he went back to his boss and asked what the golf tees were for. The boss replied by saying they are what you rest your balls on before you drive off. The young apprentice mechanic replied "bloody hell these Rolls Royce people think of everything don't they."

MR W VYSE (STOKE-ON-TRENT)

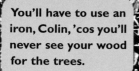

You'll have to use an iron, Colin, 'cos you'll never see your wood for the trees.

WHAT A FIND

I WAS PLAYING a round of golf with a friend. He teed off straight into the thick, rough grass. I commented that I didn't think he would be able to find his ball and advised him to play a provisional ball, just in case. "No problem," he replied. "It will be easy to find". I asked him how and he replied that the ball glows and therfore is very easy to find. Sure enough he found his ball straight away.

Later on he played a shot into some trees. I again advised him to play a provisional ball, just in case he couldn't find his "glowing" ball. "No problem," he replied. "It will be easy to find even if it's stuck up a tree because it bleeps very loudly." Sure enough he found his ball straight away.

Towards the end of our round of golf, my friend unfortunately played his ball into the pond near the Club House. I said it was a shame he had lost his "bleeping, glowing" ball, only to be corrected by him saying that his ball also floated, so he couldn't lose it - even in water. Sure enough, he retrieved his ball from the surface of the pond and carried on playing.

On finishing our round of golf, I asked him, "How expensive is one of these wonder golf balls and where can I get one?" "I don't know," he replied, "I found it".

MR M TEMME (MID GLAMORGAN)

It's Here Somewhere

The captain of a very posh golf club was notoriously tight. The Club House was situated at the top of a hill and it was decided that part of the hill should be bulldozed to enlarge the car park. One day, while the captain was watching the removal of trees and bushes, two members passed by and one said to the captain, "New ball was it?"

Mr Rusby (Northampton)

What An Anorak

I started playing golf about ten years ago, but I specifically remember the third game I ever played. I was playing a four-ball with three seasoned club players. On the 2nd hole I drove my tee shot onto the practice putting green outside the Club House. My partner informed me I had a free drop. In those days you dropped over your shoulder. The weather was poor with heavy drizzle. I wore a light anorak instead of the regular waterproof jacket. I dropped the ball over my shoulder, but when I turned round I could not find it. There was nowhere to lose it as there was only cut grass in the vicinity. The four of us searched for 5 minutes thinking there must be a hole somewhere. Finally, mystified, we had to give up as there were players behind us. For the next few holes that's all we talked about. We were all baffled as to where it could have gone. At the 9th hole the rain stopped and we all took off our waterproofs. As I rolled up my anorak I felt a lump in the hood and realised it was the lost ball. Being a novice and not wanting to be the talk of the Club House, I quietly folded it up and put it away. Occasionally my partners on that day talk about what could have happened to that ball. I suppose one day I will have to tell them.

Mr P Crangle (Sunderland)

AUBREY EBAN

‘ Golf has given
me an
understanding
of the futility
of life. ’

IT'S A DANGEROUS GAME

A PAINFUL PARTNERSHIP

THIS IS A STORY I heard about a man whom I didn't know personally, but believe it to be 100% true. It's about a man who broke his arm whilst playing golf and when asked how, this was the answer...

He had driven off from the tee and had sliced his ball near a water hazard. When he got to this ball it was on the water's edge, between the water and a pylon close to the pond. He decided to play his ball and in doing so lost his footing and his left leg was in the water. He grabbed the pylon and lifted his leg to shake the water off. This is when his playing partner thought he was getting an electric shock (because of the leg shaking), so he ran up and smacked him on his arm that was holding onto the pylon with one of his clubs, thus breaking his arm in two places.

MR M BELL (MIRFIELD, W YORKS)

IS THERE A DOCTOR IN THE HOUSE

IT WAS A BUSY Sunday lunchtime at the beautiful Hertfordshire Club and the 19th hole was packed with club members. Their wives and guests were enjoying lunch, prior to competing in the Annual Invitation Trophy. The convivial atmosphere was shattered when suddenly a distraught member rushed into the club house, puffing and panting and shouting "quickly, somebody phone for a doctor, there has been an accident, the Lady Captain has been hit by a wayward shot off the tee." At this point one of the member's guests who was leaning against the bar enjoying a well earned pint volunteered, "Don't worry, I'm a doctor, I'm sure we'll soon sort this out, whereabouts has the poor lady been hit?" "I think it was just about half way between the first and the second holes," explained the distraught member. "Good grief," said the doctor, "it doesn't leave much room for the bandage does it?"

MR B COOK (WOKING)

IT'S FORE YOU AGAIN

I WOULD LIKE to tell you about a humorous incident I witnessed at a golf tournament. It was about 5 years ago at the Royal Lytham Golf Club, when watching the Seniors Open. My friend and I had picked out the best of the bunch to follow round: Arnold Palmer, Gary Player and Bob Charles. On this particular hole two of the three found themselves behind a grass mound in the fairway, therefore making a blind shot to the green. We were standing about 20 yards short of the green. The first shot was played, followed immediately by a shout of "fore left". The ball came hurtling towards us and hit a male spectator, very close to us, on his left upper arm. This caused a cheer from the surrounding crowd and brought a smile to his own face. The man in question then moved to a position about 10 yards away for the next shot. The second shot was then played again followed by a shout of "fore left". This shot was to follow the same route as the first passing us and would you believe it, yes, the ball hit the same spectator in the very same place. The man just started to scratch his head much to the amusement of the crowd. The golf that day was OK but there is no doubt in my mind of the talking point of the day for the people who were to witness what must be a very unusual incident.

I wonder what odds would be given in the bookmakers?

MR N HOPKINSON (PRESTON, LANCS)

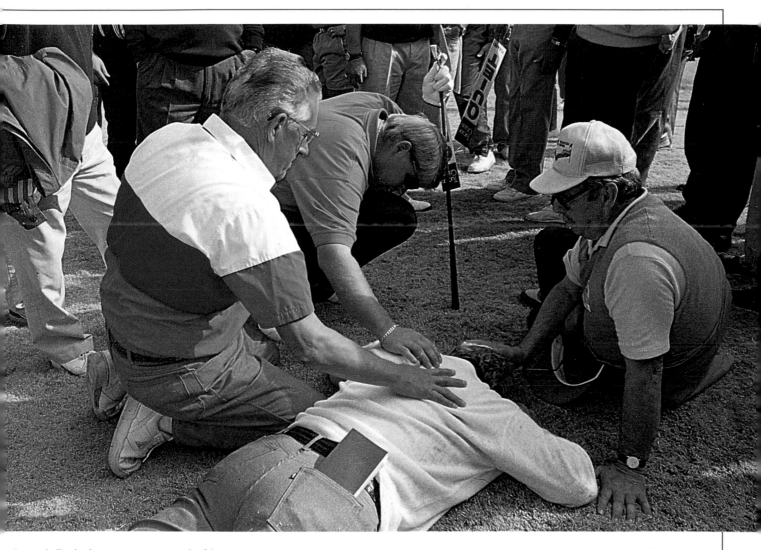

A marshall ushering spectators across the fairway, away from the tee, was unaware that John Daly was teeing-up. However, he became fully aware when Daly hit his longest drive of the day, knocking the marshall unconscious. On waking, he found Daly kneeling over him, claiming that he was an immovable obstruction, and wanted a free drop!

THERE'S A BALL OUT THERE WITH YOUR NAME ON IT

I ONCE PLAYED a round of golf with a Scotsman who had recently retired from work. During the game, every time "Fore" was shouted he dove for cover. I said to him, "It's no good ducking and diving John, if your name is on the ball, you'll get it." "I know" he replied, "that's what I'm worried about, my name is Dunlop and I'm 65 aye!"

A FINE ROUND

DURING OUR LAST golf society meeting the members introduced, as a way of raising monies for both society funds and as donations to local charities, a "fines marshall" to fine players various sums for minor misdemeanours, before, during and after the meeting. All players were on their best behaviour. I had played reasonably well during the competition, was playing the 17th hole and my second shot from just off the left hand side of the fairway. Suddenly I was hit very hard by a ball, played from the 17th tee by a so-called fellow member before we were out of range. The shot, which struck me under the armpit area, was very painful and caused me to lose balance and fall down into the rough. I came to my senses to view a sea of faces of members all expressing concern as to my well being. I quickly recovered my composure and completed my round, knowing I had not done enough to win but feeling quite pleased with my game and life in general. After a pleasant dinner and presentation, imagine my total shock when reading the "Fine Marshall's" list of fines I discovered:-

B Blakeway - fined   *Lying in the grass in the sun too long and not calling through the following group.*
Feigning a heart attack and damaging the turf by falling down.
Having an extra stroke which did not appear on his scorecard and for which he had not signed.

I paid my fines with a sly smile having noted that at the next meeting it was my turn to be "Fines Marshall".

B BLAKEWAY (WEST MIDLANDS)

WOODEN HEAD

A MEMBER OF our golf club was using his favourite 3 wood golf club which had the old type whipping securing the shaft to the club head. The hole being a par 5 and 481 yards, he now reached for the 3 wood to play his 2nd shot into the green. The club head broke from the shaft and shot up high over his head with the whipping still attached. The whipping pulled the club head sharply down and hit him on his head, temporarily stunning him. He fell to the ground in a dazed state. His playing partner rushed over and helped him to stand up. As he stood, still a little dazed, he said in a shaky voice, "That silly sod behind has driven into me."

MR E W SLADE (DEVON)

EGG HEAD

ABOUT 5 YEARS ago our golf society played Leek Golf Course. Coming up the ninth, I put my second shot into a bunker straight in front of the Club House. My mate says, "Watch the car park Foxy" (as it is not the first time I've ended up in one). "No problem" I said, very tentatively. I played my third shot, topped it and guess what? Straight into the car park. My partners were rolling about on the green so I walked to the hedge to have a look. There were BMWs, Mercedes, SAABs, sports cars and even a Roller. I thought, 'Whoops, I'm not insured.' Suddenly an old gentleman appeared and said, "Is this what you're looking for son?" holding a golf ball in his hand. I looked at it and said, "Yes, that's mine, what a relief." The gentleman said, "No harm done". I thanked him and he doffed his hat, and on his head was a lump as big as an egg.

MR P FOX (GRANTHAM, LINCS)

> **❛ The uglier a man's legs are the better he plays golf. It's almost law. ❜**
>
> H.G. WELLS

CRASHED AND BURNED

LEVEN LINKS GOLF course, adjacent to the promenade has a burn 20 yards from the first tee with a small bridge for players crossing. Many people often stand at the large mesh fence to watch the golfers drive off. A foursome took the tee one lovely summer's afternoon with a huge crowd of onlookers. The first player nervously duffed his shot which landed in the burn. The watching crowd was amused. The second player now much more aware of the crowd did exactly the same and his ball also landed in the burn. The crowd this time began to titter.

The third player was really on edge and hit his ball on the head. It trundled along the ground straight into the burn. By now the crowd was laughing and eagerly awaiting the result of the final player's drive. Much to their great disappointment he lashed a beauty right down the middle. Unable to resist his great delight and relief as he was walking away to cross the bridge over the burn he turned and shouted to the crowd, "I bet you thought I was going to duff it into the burn too!" Whereupon he missed his footing on the bridge and plunged headfirst into the burn.

MR W HENDERSON (FIFE, SCOTLAND)

CLANG CLANG CLANG GOES THE TROLLEY

IN 1994 I went on a captains trip to Knaresborough golf course. During the round on one hole I had putted out and to go to the next tee we had to go up a steep bank. As it happened that day I had hired an electric trolley for the first time. I thought the trolley would go up the bank easily but I was wrong, so I backed up and put full power on and tried again this time trotting with the trolley.

The trolley hit the bank going fairly fast but I could not keep up with it and it did a wheely on the next tee. I went flat on my face holding the handle. I was dragged across the tee with the handle digging a groove in the tee and golf clubs coming out of my bag. My playing partners were screaming with laughter. After the match. I had to stand on a beer crate and tell everybody about it.

MR D PATTERSON (LEEDS)

RIB-CRACKING LAUGHTER

I WAS PLAYING with three of my friends, as we do every Sunday. We all teed off from the first which is quite a straightforward par four. All of us had a simple chip on for our second shot, which we duly managed. As we approached the green we left our trollies by the second tee. My three friends walked up the bank which surrounds the first green, waiting for me to join them. Unfortunately, as I was walking up the bank I slipped and fell onto the head of my putter, which resulted in a cracked rib. This resulted in fits of laughter from the other three with sympathy at a minimum. However, I did manage to play on and recorded an equal best ever score of 81.

MR J OAKLEY (WEST SUSSEX)

SNAKE BITE

TWO ENGLISHMEN were on a golfing holiday in California. After having an even par round they arrive at the 18th tee. The first hits a beautiful shot down the middle of the fairway. The second, not wanting to be outdone by his partner, hits his shot as hard as he can and hooks it into the trees. While they both searched for the ball, one decides to relieve himself. Unfortunately a black snake strikes and bites his manhood, he screams to his friend, "Quick find a doctor, I've been bitten by a black snake". His friend sprints across the golf course and into the clubhouse screaming, "I need a doctor, urgently." One of the members standing at the bar answered his desperate call, "I'm a doctor, how can I help?" He told the doctor of his friend's dilemma back on the 18th fairway. "Well," said the doctor, "the only course of action is to suck out the poison." So he sprinted back to where his friend was lying in agony, screaming, "Did you find a doctor, where is he?" He replied, "I found a doctor and he said I'm afraid you're going to die."

MR S COOMBS (KENT)

I TOLD YOU SO

EVERY SUNDAY MORNING for several years my brother and myself meet to have a game of pitch and putt. Over that period many people have joined us and as a rule it's good fun. This story, however, concerns our latest guest. For several weeks he came to join us, he had several annoying habits but one that stood out was his insistence on shouting fore as the group in front walked off the green. It amused him to see people duck and cover their heads. We explained on several occasions that it's a serious call and should not be messed with, but to no avail. One particular morning, as we left the first green, a loud shout of fore went up. I automatically ducked and covered my head as did my brother. When we stood up we noticed our friend lying flat on his back. We rushed over to find blood rushing from his nose. After a while we stemmed the flow of blood. I asked how he'd been hit in the face as we were walking away from play. He said when he heard the shout fore, he thought someone was messing about, and turned to see who it was. If you're wondering if I said I told you so, of course I did.

MR P CROKE (DERBY)

OUT FORE SIX

I WAS PLAYING in a golf society at Royal Mid-Surrey one day last year. It was a very sunny day and very warm. As we played our first 18 holes I noticed a cricket pitch on the field next to the 3rd tee with a match taking place. When we started our second round in the afternoon we finally came to the 3rd tee and noticed the cricket match still taking place. When my playing partner was just about to hit his tee shot, a cricket ball came flying over the fence and hit him on the side of the head and knocked him out. A player from the cricket field then came running over and I asked, "Why didn't you shout fore." He answered, "Because it was a six."

MR D SINGER (LONDON)

> **❝ Golfers are the greatest worriers in the world of sports. In fast-action sports, like football, baseball or tennis, there is little time to worry compared to the time a golfer has on his hands between shots. ❞**
>
> BILLY CASPER JR

AND IN 20 YEARS

Helium underpants will save on shoe leather...

Motorised balls will add distance...

...and thought control will erradicate putting entirely

AT DEATH'S DOOR

GRAVE SHOT

IN 1967 I was playing in a foursome at Sanford golf club, North Carolina, USA. At the 16th hole, a par 4 right hand dog leg, my partner Doc Archer sliced his drive over the bushes separating the course from the town cemetery. The ball landed in a partly dug grave, about 20 ft from a nearby grave, around which a funeral party was gathered. Because our game determined that all lies be played, irrespective of circumstance (which did lead to some wonderful scoring at times and negated all handicapping systems), Doc climbed through the bushes and over the fence, carrying his pitching wedge. Finding the ball on a pile of soil in an uphill lie, he took a cramped stance, short backswing and managed to lift the ball out and to within 10 feet of the hole. Climbing out of the grave he faced the mourners who by now were surreptitiously watching him, while the priest intoned, Doc removed his cap, bowed slightly and with dignified strides returned to the course. Putting out for a birdie three he took a dollar off the other three of us, which for someone who played back from the dead was a small reward.

MR J POOLEY (ECCLES, LANCS)

A MARK OF RESPECT

JIMMY AND TAM were playing the 12th hole near the main road. As Jimmy was about to putt, a hearse was passing. Jimmy stopped, took off his cap, and bowed his head. Tam said, "I've been a member here for 25 years, and it's the first time I've seen anyone show such respect to a hearse passing." Jimmy responded, "It's the least I could do, after all, I was married to her for 42 years."

MR A MCNEIL (GLASGOW)

HEART-FELT ACTIONS

ALL MEMBERS of the club rushed outside when the sight of two golfers lugging three trolleys and carrying a third man between them, went past the clubhouse window.

John, one of the golfers, bedraggled and absolutely knackered gasped in between great gulps for breath, "quick, call an ambulance - it's old Joe, he had a heart attack on the 6th hole and we've had to carry him in."

"But why is he so filthy?" asked the Secretary, looking down at the limp form on the floor, covered in mud, leaves and other debris. "Ah well", explained John, "we had to put him down to take our shots on the way in."

MR D HOLT (ROCHDALE, LANCS)

OLD GOLFERS NEVER DIE

MY FATHER, who was very much a ladies man, his extra-marital antics not unknown to his friends, was also a keen golfer playing off a handicap of 8. He was recovering from an illness, and friends sent the usual get well cards, one of which said "Old golfers never die, they just lose their balls."

My father's reply to the female sender was "Dear Madge, many thanks for your concern over my balls, but they have been in that much rough over the years, they know their own way home now."

MR B GATEHOUSE (POOLE, DORSET)

HEAD SHOT

A MAN WHO is playing golf with his wife and slices his tee shot into an adjacent backyard. The wife points out that he can hit the ball back through the barn and onto the fairway. He tries this but the ball ricochets off a rafter, hits his wife in the head and kills her.

Several years later the man is playing the same hole with a pal, and once again he sliced into the barnyard. The pal says, "You can get back to the fairway if you hit it through the barn." The first man says, "No the last time I tried that I bogeyed the hole."

MR R MARTIN (SLOUGH, BERKS)

GOLF RAGE

IT'S IN THE BAG

WHILST PLAYING at one of our local courses I watched the antics of a fellow in a foursome ahead of us. They were playing across a wide lake and this fellow put about 6 or 7 consecutive balls into the lake. His frustration got the better of him so he did no more. Being a big chap, he lifted his clubs, bag and trolley above his head and dumped the lot into the lake before storming off the course vowing never to play again. His colleagues then carried on without him and we moved on behind them. Just as we were playing the same lake the big fellow returned to our amazement, walked into the lake, up to his waist where he had previously ditched his gear. My friend shouted to him, "Have you changed your mind then?" "No" he said, "my car keys are in the bloody bag."

MR T GRIFFITHS (SOMERSET)

DIVOT HEAD

I WAS PLAYING in a threesome with some friends at my local golf club in the monthly medal competition. One of my friends who was playing with us was a chap called Joe. He wasn't playing at his Sunday best and he's the sort of person who gets very irate and emotional if things aren't going his way. By the eighth green he was just about ready to explode as he had just four putted the par four hole which he had practically driven on his tee shot.

We then approached the ninth hole, a short par three of 120 yards. It was Joe's turn to tee off, and using a wedge he shanked his tee shot out of bounds into the nearby cornfield. He then went bananas!

While he was hacking away madly with his wedge at the ground he took a huge divot which flew about ten yards up into the air and came down straight on top of his head! We laughed so much, we were unable to continue the round.

MR J EDDY (CORNWALL)

**6 The least thing upset him on the links. He missed short putts
because of the uproar of butterflies in the adjoining meadows. 9**

P. G. WODEHOUSE

THE ITALIAN JOB

RECENTLY MY FRIEND and I travelled to Dundee. The main objective was to visit some of his family, especially his mother who at that time had not been well. Of secondary importance was to play golf. This we managed to do by spending days at Forfar and Camberdown Park. It was after one of these outings that we ended up in one of the local bars and met some of my friend's old acquaintances. Invariably the conversation soon got round to golf. Jamie recalled how he was asked to caddy at the Downfield golf club, a former championship course in Dundee, in an international youth tournament. His employer was a young Italian golfer, Angelo. During the first round all seemed to be going well between caddy and player but Jamie had started to sense the Italian's frustration as he bogeyed rather than birdied. The relationship took a turn for the worse on the ninth hole. Angelo: "How far?" Jamie: "158 yards, wind coming from the right. Take a five iron."

This information was accepted and a shot taken. It was not struck perfectly and the ball plummeted into the greenside bunker at the front. At this point the five iron took on the guise of the rotary blades of a Westland helicopter as it disappeared through the air accompanied by a tirade of Italian expletives. The Italian's behaviour and petulance then began to break the normally well composed and tolerant Jamie. The atmosphere, now strained, was about to deteriorate further as they reached the 15th hole.

Angelo: "How far?"

Jamie: "161 yards"

Angelo: "Give me a 5 iron"

Jamie: "I can't"

Angelo "Why not?"

Jamie: "You haven't got one"

Angelo: "What do you mean I haven't got one?"

Jamie: "Don't you remember you threw it away - I didn't think you wanted it."

At this point Jamie sensed an Italian eruption was imminent and beat a hasty retreat to the sanctuary of the 19th hole, leaving the Italian to stomp off up the fairway with bag slung over sunken shoulders.

MR L SALTER (CARTERTON, OXON)

You'll never cut it down with that, Seve.

CELEBRITY GOLFERS

The true definition of a golfer is one who shouts 'Fore', takes five, and puts down a three.

When you are playing golf, nothing counts like your opponent.

Golf liars have one advantage over fishing liars – they don't have to show anything to prove it.

❛ I'd give up golf if I didn't have so many jumpers. ❜

BOB HOPE

❛ Excuse me, Madam, would you mind either standing back or closing your mouth – I've lost four balls already. ❜

TED RAY, COMEDIAN, TO A SPECTATOR

❛ It's good sportsmanship to not pick up lost golf balls while they are still rolling. ❜

MARK TWAIN

GLEN CAMPBELL: SAID OF PLAYING
WITH FELLOW MUSICIAN CHARLEY PRIDE

*❛ I only see Charley when we get to
the greens. Charley hits some good
woods – trouble is most of them
have leaves on. ❜*

*❛ And now here's
Jack Lemmon,
about to hit that
all-important
eighth shot. ❜*

TV COMMENTATOR
AS LEMMON PLAYED
THE FOURTEENTH
HOLE AT PEBBLE
BEACH

ONE FLEW OVER THE GOLF COURSE

SEA BIRDIE

IT WAS SUNDAY 24 June 1995 at North Wales Golf Club in Llandudno. On arrival at the club the heavens opened and thunder and lightning streaked across the course causing a three hour delay. By the time we reached the third green the rain returned and the wind was that strong it was blowing the clubs and trolley over. The conditions continued throughout the round. On reaching the 18th tee I thought to myself, 'the weather's been bad, my golf has been poor, at least I've reached the 18th tee.' I struck a perfect drive to the middle of the fairway. Feeling much better, my second shot went to the right onto the first fairway. I was about 50 yards from my ball when a seagull picked it up and flew off with it towards the first green with me chasing it. The seagull dropped the ball 100 yards further on. My partner was doubled up with laughter and through the speeches I was reminded I'd had a birdie.

MR H MORL (CHESTER)

EATING CROW

WHILST PLAYING the 6th hole at Barnhurst golf club I witnessed the longest drive I've ever seen on the 7th. The gentleman negotiated an avenue of trees and left himself a 9 iron to the green. As he strolled, chest out, towards his superdrive a crow swooped and flew away towards the third with his ball. The crow soared over 50 ft trees, chased by the owner of the ball whose composure had drained away to be replaced by insanity. Other players who missed the incident assumed the poor fellow had gone mad. The feathered black thief comfortably escaped. One assumes the golfer no longer uses 'top flite' balls.

MR J GARLINGE (WELLING, KENT)

BYE BYE BLACKBIRD

MY BOYFRIEND WILL and I, went for a short break to visit his sister, Frances and her husband Peter, who live in Enfield, Middlesex. We had taken our golf clubs because Peter said he would arrange for us to have a game of golf with himself and his father. We went one late afternoon for a round in the twilight session. We came to the 14th hole and I teed off, and next to go was Will. He stands 6' 4" and weighs around 14 stone, so you can imagine he really hits a ball with some power. Will hit his shot from the 14th. Just as it started to climb, a lone blackbird flew straight into the path of his ball and was killed instantly. Poor Will just stood there in shock as did the rest of us. Feathers were floating down all around us, when Peter turned to Will and said "I'll mark that a birdie at the fourteenth."

MRS I J BROUGHTON (GRIMSBY)

TIME TO CROW

BEING A FORMER seafarer and a very keen golfer I have been very privileged to have played on some of the most beautiful courses in the world. I was purser of the P&Q ship Canton in 1955 and amongst the passengers was a representative of the company's agents in the Far East, also a keen golfer. We played on the Hong Kong course and at the short hole both drives landed on the green, my ball some 30 ft away and my friend's ball even further. As he was about to putt, a crow swooped down picked up his ball and dropped it an inch away from the pin. Needless to say he won the hole.

MR L WYETH (LINCS)

PARROT FASHION

WHILST HAVING a round on one of our local municipal courses, in ideal conditions, bright sunny skies, golf going very well indeed, my partner and myself playing up to the green on the 6th came across what we thought was a heart attack case. This chap was laid flat out. We dashed across ready to give mouth to mouth, but much to our surprise this guy was trying to catch a parrot. When asked what he was supposed to be doing, he said this is one birdie he did not want to miss as he could get £500 for it.

I dived at the parrot, grabbed it with both hands, and tried to put it into my bag. The parrot had other ideas. It opened its rock hard beak and commenced to crack my thumb. Panic set in, people around were shouting don't let go but what they didn't know was the bloody thing would not let go. It hung on with its beak locked firmly closed.

To add to my painful and alarming situation it had a mate which joined in the action. Swooping low, it dived at me, trying to crack my skull. After getting free from the hooked-beak demon I commenced to play golf, but was bombarded and hassled by these two birds all the way down the 7th fairway. Incidentally, the birds had escaped from the local park aviaries the week before. This I might say is the first and last time I have had two birdies in one game.

L G CUMINS (EAST YORKS)

By Rook Or By Crook

MY STORY is based on a golf society aptly named after the local pub - the Lancashire Fold in Middleton, Manchester. The story concerns a week's golfing holiday in Perranporth, Cornwall, consisting of twenty-four men aged from twenty-two up to sixty years of age. On arrival we made our way to the accommodation which was six large static caravans situated in the middle of the golf course. After travelling down on the Saturday the golf competition began on the Monday through to Friday, with a variation of competitions to find a winner at the end of the week. Myself and three other players who were sharing a caravan decided to divide the winnings equally whatever the outcome.

After four days of great golf, sunshine and very late nights, myself and my friends were well positioned in the top ten. It was only then, on the eve of the final day while walking back to the caravan, that something crossed my mind. All week I had noticed there were a lot of large black rooks flying around the seaside links and what I thought would be a bit of fun turned out to be in our favour. Just after everybody had settled for the evening, I got up, dressed and left the caravan holding my ammunition - a loaf of bread. I tore the bread into pieces and scattered it over the roofs of the other five caravans. I then returned for a good nights sleep, everyone else unaware of what I had done.

The next morning everybody met for breakfast, my lips were tightly sealed. I could not help but notice the bags underneath people's eyes. Then the questions began - who was walking up and down the caravan roofs in the middle of the night? Only I knew it was the rooks on the fibreglass surface. No one else the wiser, the day's final competition began with everyone feeling weary and tired from lack of sleep. It just so happened that at the end of the week's golf, myself and three others in the caravan finished in the top five, sharing the biggest winnings. We celebrated that evening with several beers.

MR M WINDOW (MANCHESTER)

Back To The Crow's Nest

A CUNNING THIEF is plaguing members of Cleveland golf club with about ten raids a day. Members know the identity of the culprit who swoops in broad daylight but they are powerless to stop the spree. A crooked crow is stealing golf balls from the Redcar course and has already swiped between 50 and 70 balls. Captain of the club Peter Gray says it hangs around the 2nd and 17th holes waiting for easy pickings. It waits for the tee shot then swoops down, picks up the balls and flies off. It was extremely funny at first but now members are getting a bit annoyed. Member, Ron Towers, from Redcar said the crow was getting members' feathers ruffled. 'My friend thought it was stealing white ones so he used a yellow ball - it got that as well.' A spokesman for Cleveland Police said "I suspect the perpetrator is crowing with delight at his success but I'm sure the golfers would like to see it crow-ned."

MR R TOWERS (REDCAR)

❛ At times it is the greatest game in the world and sometimes it's sadder than a death in the family. ❜

ANON

MAJOR MISHAP

MAJOR GILES ADDRESSED his ball on the first tee. It was a lovely summer's morning and he was playing in his usual four ball. As he drew the club back he was thinking "that's it, nice and slow, wait for the sweet sound of a perfect hit and the applause that normally follows from my colleagues" but no applause came, only the sound of breaking glass and guffaws of laughter from his playing partners. The Major realised he had sliced the ball at an acute angle straight through the green-keeper's cottage window some 100 yards away. The Major looked round anxiously to see if there were any other witnesses other than his now hysterical friends. Having satisfied himself that no one else had witnessed the disastrous event, he quickly teed up another ball and immediately topped it 100 yards up the fairway. By the fourth hole the joke had worn thin and after the Major had promised each a large scotch after the game, his friends promised not to mention the matter again (well at least not in front of him). Despite his 11 at the first hole, by this time the Major was back in form and playing to his 12 handicap. The remainder of the round went without incident and at the 18th all players shook hands after a close encounter, which the Major and his partner won 2 and 1.

Walking back to the clubhouse the Major was approached by a uniformed police officer. Taking him to one side, the stern looking officer said "Excuse me sir, are you the gentleman who put a golf ball through the green-keeper's cottage window?" The Major was an honest man and decided to come clean. "Well officer, yes unfortunately I was," he said, head bowed like a naughty schoolboy. "Well sir, I'm afraid I have some unfortunate news for you, apparently the green keeper has only been married a week and he and his young wife were in the middle of how shall we say a bit of how's your father."

"That's terrible" interrupted the Major. "Yes it is rather," continued the officer, "he should have been sorting out the irrigation problem on the 7th green at the time. Anyway your ball hit 'Wentworth' the green-keeper's dog on the head and in its dizzy state the dog lashed onto the green-keeper's, how shall we say equipment leaving him in considerable discomfort. He is as we speak undergoing emergency surgery." The Major was now in a sorry state and clasping his forehead he slumped to the ground muttering "Oh God how awful, tell me officer what can I do?" The policeman looked at him for a moment and replied, "It seems to me Sir you could adjust your grip, not stand so close to the ball and maybe consider a couple of lessons with the Club Pro."

MR R DAVISON (COVENTRY)

Oh please, let it be my thumb.

DON'T MIND US

ONE DAY, WHEN I was a boy of 10, my dad said to me "Son do you fancy a round of golf as my caddy on Saturday, I am playing in a local medal competition." I promptly agreed and on Saturday morning I was up at 7 am too excited to think of anything else but carrying my dad's clubs round in a competition. We made our way up to the Golf Club and my dad signed himself in. I was as proud as punch carrying those clubs about, until that is we made our way up to the first tee. My dad was playing with a friend of his, a local tradesman like himself, who teed off first and hit a nice drive down the middle of the fairway. Now it was my dad's turn. I don't know really how to describe my dad's swing, but if you can imagine a man in a field cutting corn with a sythe then you would not be far away. Anyway, my dad teed up, and jokingly said "I hope there is nobody in the clubhouse as I slice to the right." Everybody laughed because the clubhouse was protected by a 14ft high fence and was about 100 yards to the right of the tee. My father swung at the ball which went veering off to the right, clearing the fence, through a skylight glass panel and promptly embedded itself in the lounge area of the clubhouse.

To add to the total embarrassment I was suffering, my dad said "come on now son, let's go and survey the situation." We walked into the clubhouse, the ball was sitting beside some people who had just sat down for a pint and a toastie. The steward of the club came across to my dad and said "would you like me to open the sliding double doors so you can play your shot?" Which he did. I gave my father a 7 iron and he played his second shot. We made our way down the first tee and finally finished the hole with a 10. My dad then went on for a further 3 holes and in a mutual agreement with his partner retired to the 19th hole for refreshments.

MR A BOYD (STRANRAER)

GET A GRIP

IT SEEMED LIKE such a simple task to wander around the local golf shop in order to find myself a new driver, but unfortunately it did not quite work out that way. It was the final day of the British Open 1995 and the manager of the store was sat behind the counter watching the action on a television when I arrived at the shop. I didn't know exactly what I was looking for, I just wanted a new club as the one I was using was second hand. As I browsed a young lad approached me to see if I required any assistance and I asked him what he thought to clubs with graphite shafts. As our conversation developed, he asked me if I would like to go to the fitting room to give a couple of clubs a practice swing in order to see which sort I preferred. I agreed and he asked permission from the manager and selected two or three clubs for me to try.

"To begin with sir, we'll see how fast your swing is. I'll just place this magic eye on the floor behind you and then you take a swing." So I swung the club as instructed and waited for the results. "It hasn't picked that up correctly, don't be frightened of it, you can't do any damage. Just imagine the flag is in the middle of that wall." As instructed I swung again, the club slipped straight out of my hand, hurtled across the room and went straight through a plate glass cabinet in the corner. "Why did you let go?" shouted a very pale assistant. "I'm sorry, I didn't let go on purpose, it slipped out of my hands," I replied in my defence. By this point there were a few heads appearing round the corner to see what was happening and I could feel myself turning from pale pink to bright red with embarrassment. We both just stood there, speechless and looked at the devastation. "Why did you let go?" he said again, and then again, in total disbelief. I felt like pointing out that it was he who had said that I couldn't harm anything, but he already looked close to tears. The manager eventually approached and I apologised again. I didn't really know what else to say but he was only concerned for my welfare as glass had flown everywhere. The poor lad was ushered away to find a brush and a vacuum cleaner before anyone was hurt. I couldn't help but think that maybe I'd curtailed a very promising career. The manager picked the club out of the remnants of the cabinet. The head resembled a hedgehog, embedded with glass, and the graphite shaft was more like rubber. "I don't suppose you've got another one?" I hesitantly enquired. "I quite liked it!" The manager just shook his head and apologised as he turned to return to the television. On his way out he stopped and looked at the gauge on the floor, "if it's any consolation," he said, "your swing speed is about 94 miles an hour". The poor cabinet didn't stand a chance.

MR M WHITEHEAD (LEEDS)

> **6 My worst day on the golf course still beats my best day in the office. 9**
>
> JOHN HALLISEY

TWO BRICKS SHORT OF A LOAD

THREE OF US were playing in a medal round at Norwich. On the seventh tee the best line to take was a large brick factory chimney in the distance. Michael, who was Irish, informed us that they were going to knock it down. Brian said it would be best if they left the top 20 ft up. Michael said "Oh no, they are knocking it all down."

MR G PARR (CHORLEY)

FORE WARNED

TWO IRISHMEN strolling on a golf course stepped from behind some bushes onto the fairway, there was a shout of fore and as they ducked a ball whistled past their heads. Retreating behind the bushes they waited and as one of them made to continue walking his friend warned him, "Don't go out there yet Pat, there's another 3 balls to come yet."

MR M FORBES (ABERDEEN)

Trousers are now allowed to be worn by ladies on the course. But they must be removed before entering the clubhouse.

SIGN AT IRISH GOLF CLUB

8th Hole, The
European Club, Brittas
Bay, Ireland.

GOLF DEBUNKERED

I WENT TO WATCH a golf tournament in Suffolk a few years ago and met two very friendly Irishmen who were on holiday. It soon became apparent that they had never seen golf played and had no idea of the point of the game. They walked with me as we followed the first pairing down the first fairway. The second player's drive had come to rest in a deep bunker just short of the green. He stepped in, took an almighty swing with his wedge. Sand came out in a huge cloud but the ball stayed firmly in the bunker. After 5 or 6 more hefty clouts the sand was everywhere which the Irishmen found highly amusing. Eventually the ball popped out onto the green to great applause especially from my two friends. After two putts the ball fell into the hole and the Irishmen gasped. "Oh no," said one, "now he'll have one hell of a job playing it out of there."

MR K CANSDALE (CLACTON ON SEA)

MOLE HOLE

AN EXCLUSIVE GOLF club was having problems with a mole digging up the 18th green outside the clubhouse window. They hired an Irish pest exterminator to catch the mole and to subject it to extreme pain before destroying it. The captain enquired whether or not the mole has been caught and was told - "Yes, I caught it yesterday and remembered what you said about pain, I buried it alive."

MR W YOUNG (TYNE AND WEAR)

COLOUR BLIND

PAT AND MICK were playing a par three hole and they could just see the top of the flag. Pat teed off and hit a good shot followed by an equally good shot from Mick. When they arrived on the green they could see one ball on the lip of the hole and the other ball in the hole, "what ball were you playing?" asked Pat. Mick replied "I was playing a Slazenger no. 1."

"So was I" said Pat and they could not decide which of their balls was in the hole. They decided to call over the Secretary to resolve the problem. When he was told what had occurred he burst out laughing and said, "Come on, lads, which one of you was playing the yellow ball?"

MR M GRAYTHORNE (LEICESTER)

> **6** Certainly they [the greens] are the greenest, which is hardly surprising in a country where housewives habitually peep out of their cottage windows and observe that it is a beautiful day for hanging the washing out to rinse. **9**

PETER DOBEREINER

UP ON THE ROOF

PADDY AND MICHAEL were repairing the club house roof and watched bemused as a rookie hacked his way up the 18th - never once on the fairway. He went from trees to rough to bunkers and 15 shots later managed to get to the green. Three putts later the ball vanished into the hole. "He'll never get it out of there" said Paddy.

MR P HEADLAND (NORTHANTS)

17th hole,
Ballybunion Golf
Club, Ireland

AGE OLD STORIES

IN MY DAY...

WHILST SITTING in the busy locker room cleaning up his clubs before his daily round the old man sat silent, contemplating another round on his local course when suddenly the door creeks open and in walks Seve Ballesteros looking for someone to give him a game. "Anybody want to play me today?" asks Seve to which none of the members reply.

The old man stands up and says, "I'm just about to go out, I'll give you a game."

Seve starts to laugh. "Listen old man, I'm looking for a decent game and I also play for money."

"So do I," replies the old man.

Seve says "I'm talking about real money, not your £1 a hole sort of game."

The old man says, "OK then, how does £1,000 per hole sound?"

"Fine old man, let's go then". So they head off to the first tee...

After seventeen pulsating holes of birdies and pars both men walk onto the eighteenth tee, even with all to play for. As Seve won the previous hole he tees up first. The eighteenth hold is a dog leg right with 40 foot high trees guarding the green. Seve weighs up the options, goes into his bag, and pulls out his three iron for safety. Just before he hits the old man says with a smirk on his face, "Hey son, I can remember the days when I could reach this green with a good drive." Seve looks at him and senses a fresh challenge. He delves back into his bag, puts away his three iron, and pulls out his driver. He aims for the green and strikes it as hard as he can. He hits it right on line but it clips a tree just short of the green and falls out of bounds. The old man pulls out a three iron from his bag. He strikes it perfectly to the heart of the fairway just past the elbow of the dog leg. Seve, feeling under great pressure now, goes with the driver again. Again he clips the trees and goes out of bounds. He then turns to the old man and says, "Hey old man, you've never hit that green with a drive in your life have you?" The old man starts to laugh and says, "Aye son, but that was forty years ago, before those trees were planted." The old man walks to his ball, hits an iron to the heart of the green, two putts and wins the match.

MR G SHANKLAND (GLASGOW)

A GAME TO GET YOUR TEETH INTO

I WAS PLAYING in a fourball match with an old chap, aged 71 years, named Harry Renton. He could not hit the ball very far but was an absolutely excellent chipper and putter. We just managed to tie the match on eighteen and at the first extra hole our opponents both put their second shots in the bunker. I had gone out of bounds. Harry hit two good shots and chipped to about two feet. One of our opponents was quite close to the hole but the other had not escaped from the bunker. Their ball was slightly behind Harry's, so they putted first and sank the putt. I was confident Harry would hole for a half. He stood over the putt, then stood back and suddenly let out a big sneeze at which point the top set of his false teeth flew out and hit the ball. What a way to lose!

MR S SANDERS (BRISTOL)

In his early days, Seve would throw balls into the woods to practice. Years later he won tournaments barely hitting a fairway.

WHAT A PAIR

OLD ALBERT GOES in one day to see the Golf Club Secretary, "Mr Secretary, just to let you know I have decided to resign my membership this year."

"I am very sorry to hear that Albert, what's the problem?"

"Well it's the damn eyesight you know, at 83 it's deteriorating so rapidly that even the strongest specs can't help, soon as I hit the ball I can't see it, complete waste of time."

"Don't despair Albert, we have a new member, Henry, just moved into the area, he's 97, A1 eyesight, doesn't even wear specs. I'll pair you with him in Saturday's medal, he can keep an eye on your ball for you!" "Splendid Mr Secretary, thank you ever so much."

There they are on Saturday morning 10am on the first tee. Albert steps up, hits his drive away. "Did you see it Henry?" "Yes Albert". "Where did it go?" I can't remember!"

M LYNSKEY (SOLIHULL)

**❛ Well done
Seve, i knew
if we kept at
it you'd hit a
fairway. ❜**

Seve Ballesteros
and Jose Maria
Olazabal on the
18th hole, Ryder
Cup 1991, Kiawah
Island.

ACCURACY IS ALL

WHILST WALKING ALONG the 5th fairway of my local course, I met a man, gloomily marking down yardage distances. I got speaking to him and it transpired that he was a caddy for a professional playing in the Ulster PGA. He told me that the pro was so irate about his erratic performance in the first round that he blamed the caddy for getting the yardage wrong. He demanded that the caddy went out onto the course and recalculate his yardage distances. I told him that I had the solution, in my profession as a Civil Engineer I had a Distance Wheel in my possession and it could be accurate to 0.001 of an inch. The caddy seemed unimpressed and replied, "No, he'll bloody kill me, if the distances aren't spot on."

MR L BISHOP (CO DOWN)

ALWAYS PROTECT YOUR EQUIPMENT

FOLLOWING A VERY enthusiastic round of crazy golf, beating my sister-in-law on the last hole, I thought that I should really try my hand at the local, newly opened Golf Club. Fees paid, complete with a compulsory course of six lessons with the Golf Pro, I presented myself at the Driving Range. I could almost read the Pro's mind as he cast his eye over the assorted set of clubs, that I fished out of a very old and worn club bag discarded by a neighbour whilst clearing his garage out. The Pro placed a ball on the mat, stood back and invited me to hit it, whenever I felt ready. For the first 15 minutes, but it seemed like 30, I swung at the ball trying in vain to make some sort of contact. My language at this time was to say the least colourful as I accused it of moving, cheating, of being fatherless and worse!!

I finally made contact with the blasted thing with what I know now as a No. 4 Iron and made a near perfect left angled shot. The all knowing Golf Pro, with an annoying, irritating smirk on his face made a suggestion to correct this "fault". I eventually proceeded to hit a not-so-perfect right angled shot - shots I still make but know now as a hook and a slice.

It was at this point that the Pro asked, due to my obvious ability to perform this well known 90 degree sideways shot, if I had any oriental connections. Hurt and humiliated, I decided there and then that there was definitely a similarity between me and Nick Faldo!! The next connection, although late in the lesson, was a cracker - literally!!! The ball hit the concrete wall of the range, flew off to the left striking a metal stanchion, bounced off that at speed, hitting the Pro in his nether regions. He collapsed into a heap moaning and groaning. Serves the sarcastic sod right I thought, gathering my assorted equipment together to make a quick exit. There was no way I was volunteering to look at, least of all try to treat that sort of injury!!

MR D PEACE (REDDITCH)

No humorous caption; no trick photography. This genuinely is Nick Faldo looking for his ball on the 14th at Pebble Beach. Feel better now?

‘ So tell me, Greg, <u>did</u> losing the masters like that affect your confidence at all? ’

THE ART OF MISSING

IT WAS THE LOCAL golf club charity match day and in the time honoured tradition the club professional was partnering the captain's wife. The captain's wife, whilst full of enthusiasm and willingness to learn, had not really got to grips with the game after numerous lessons. Having played six holes on all of which the captain's wife had put the pro into all sorts of trouble, he decided it was time to change the strategy. He had brilliantly driven the ball down the middle of the 7th fairway, leaving the captain's wife with a 120 yard shot to the green, over a large pond.

Knowing full well she would put the ball straight into the water he called her over and whispered, "play an air shot".

"I beg your pardon," she said. "Miss the ball," he said. "If you play an air shot it will be my turn to play and I will put the ball onto the green for you to putt."

"Are you sure?" asked the captain's wife. "Quite" said the pro. "OK, if you say so," she replied. The captain's wife surveyed the ball and very professionally inspected the lie. She then stepped back, looking up towards the green as if gauging the distance. Having deliberated, she calmly walked over to the pro and asked, "Do you think I should use an 8 or 9 iron?"

MR P WRAY (ESSEX)

CADDY SHACK CHAT

I AM AN EX-CADDY and was working at Wilmslow in the now defunct Cold Shield Windows event. All the Southport caddies used to meet at a transport cafe near the course for breakfast. In the first round there were headlines in the paper about Ken Brown missing a putt and while walking off the green he tossed his ball in the air and smashed it into the car park nearby and damaged a car. Brian Waites, his playing partner reported him to the PGA.

Alfie Tyles, Tom Watson's caddy was Ken Brown's caddy that day. The papers reported that Alfie told the PGA that he had been replacing the flagstick and didn't see the incident. Loyalty to his man. I was having breakfast with Alf and asked if he saw it. Alf replied, "It was the only shot he had hit off the middle of the club all day."

MR J MEE (LIVERPOOL)

TEACHER'S PET

THE COMPANY I used to work for had a golf society which I was keen to join but had only previously played on pitch and putt courses. I managed to borrow a half set of clubs and made off to find someone to play with. Dave volunteered, saying as an average player he could offer me some valuable tips. I had my cheap rubber golf shoes, borrowed clubs and the all important glove, although Dave said this didn't matter for a first timer, and of course plenty of balls. Equipped enough to enter the big league, I made off to the first tee. I was nervous as there were a half dozen or so golfers behind us on a bench waiting for us to go. Dave set himself on the tee giving me a commentary as he went through his routine. "Start with a 3 iron, relax, take your time, stay composed, then give it plenty of welly."

He swung the club with great gusto, completely missed the ball. The club slipped from his grasp and went perfectly 50 yards down the middle of the fairway. Casually, he turned to me, took my club and played his ball all of 30 yards, 2 inches off the ground and straight under a temporary tee. I turned away in hysterical embarrassment to see the waiting golfers in fits of laughter. We did eventually finish the round of this par 72 course, 5 other pairs had to play through. Dave looked for his ball on various holes. On the 7th hole Dave managed to hit the ball off the tee at right angles, straight between his legs and land 6 inches from the flag on the green we had just vacated. Final score for the round: Dave, the teacher, 128; me, the pupil, 96.

MR P EVANS (BOLTON, LANCS)

ANIMAL ATTRACTION

POODLE POWER

TONY BOUGHT A set of golf clubs and sought the services of a local pro. After a course of lessons he decided to apply for membership at a club we will call Ponty. This was accepted. He approached three friends who regularly play on a Sunday to ascertain if they would consider him to make up a four ball. With great trepidation they agreed. It was a hot summer's day just before noon. Tables and chairs were arranged on the clubhouse patio. These were occupied by members enjoying a drink in the sunshine, watching the finishers on the 18th. The scene is now set.

"The Williams party please", called the starter. This was Tony's group. Partners had already been agreed and Tony was to tee off last. Two good drives down the middle and one slightly pulled but in good shape. Now it was Tony's turn. He stood on the tee, placed his ball with the name facing forward. He had remembered the pro telling him to do that. He took his address position and prayed that it would go down the middle. With knees knocking, heart pounding and stomach churning he let fly. He felt everyone was watching him. They were.

A click as metal driver hits surlyn cover and the ball flies. Unfortunately it only lifted some 12 inches off the ground and was heading directly for the ladies tee and the board giving the ladies distance and index. The ball hit this board with tremendous velocity and flew off towards the 18th green and club patio. Sitting at a table with three friends enjoying a drink was the Lady Captain. Under the table lay her Standard Poodle freshly bathed and clipped sleeping in the midday sun. Little did it realise that its world was about to explode.

The ball still travelling at great speed made a bee-line for the dog and caught it squarely on the rear end. With an almighty yelp, it ran out from under the table. Unfortunately its lead had been tied to the leg of the table. Its sudden movement made the table follow in the same direction. The drinks that had been on the table flew into the air and onto the Lady Captain's new dress. In either panic or fright she jumped up and in the process pushed her chair backwards. A domino effect ensued with tables, chairs and drinks all ending up on the floor. Tony's ball finally came to rest just off the patio in some short grass.

He walked to his ball, looked at the carnage he had created and said to the Lady Captain, "excuse me, I'm new here. Do I play my ball from here or must I take three off the tee?" It is not appropriate to print the reply but it is framed in the clubhouse.

MR C HOLT (LINCOLN)

DOG GONE

WHEN TEEING OFF at our local golf course from the first tee, there is a hedge running close to the fairway down the right hand side. I took a driver from the bag. I gave the ball a mighty whack, only to slice my shot over the hedge, lost ball! Taking another shot (three off the tee) I promptly did the same again. For the third time of teeing off I thought it won't happen again, so playing with caution I took an eight iron. Just knocking it up the fairway a short distance nice and straight so I wouldn't lose another ball. But lo and behold what happened? The ball travelled 100 yards or so up the middle of the fairway. I said to myself, "thank goodness I hadn't lost this ball". Before I could proceed up the fairway for the next shot a Jack Russell Terrier ran from behind the hedge where I had previously already lost two balls and ran off with my third ball. I was told afterwards that the field behind the hedge was private and this dog was trained to take balls back through the hedge to its owner who was collecting them and selling them back to the unlucky golfers.

MR M GOWER (DUNSTABLE)

IF YOU WANT TO SUCCEED ON THE PRO CIRCUIT...

KEEP FIT...

KEEP CALM...

CREATURE COMFORTS

MY HUSBAND, Danny was teeing off the 4th, he had just hit the ball and was watching where the it had landed. When he looked down at his club, there was a blue budgerigar perched on the end. My husband thought he was seeing things (due to too many drinks the night before) until his friend laughed and the bird flew off.

On the next hole, he lost his ball in the rough and was swinging his club from side to side looking for the ball, when a squirrel ran up his club, up his arm and onto his shoulder and jumped on a tree. When he got back to the clubhouse they were all laughing their heads off and calling him Dr Doolittle.

MRS G QUINN (REIGATE, SURREY)

IT'S A VET'S LIFE

HAVING PLAYED a round of 18 holes in a veterans competition we were on our way to the car park to leave our clubs in our cars before retiring to the 19th hole for the usual refreshment. Two other gentlemen were putting their clubs into their cars when one of them asked who was the society who had just come off. I told him, 'we are the Arrow Park Vets'. His immediate reply was "Oh, I could do with a chat with one of those. My dog is suffering with stomach cramps."

MR P FLAHERTY (WIRRAL)

CREATURE DIS-COMFORTS

MANY YEARS AGO when I was young and foolish, myself and three work colleagues played golf every Sunday. We would awake at unbelievable hours and over the years covered the length and breadth of Scotland. One Sunday we went to Beith golf course for the first time. It was a nine hole course and as we arrived it was evident we were the first on the course that morning. Sheep roamed the fairways and bird song filled the air. Leaving our donations in the money box provided on the side of the unmanned starter box we moved to the first tee. The hole was an uphill par 5 and as usual we tossed a coin for sides.

I won the honour and teed off with my usual first hole trundler. Graham was next and although there was a sheep grazing, rear toward us, about 80 yards from the tee, he decided to play. He was a big stocky lad and cracked a screamer straight as a die and about 3 feet from the ground. It struck the sheep in the middle of its backside, prompting the poor creature off at a speed that would not have disgraced a greyhound. Graham's ball was nowhere to be seen.

He played a provisional and off he went up the fairway, concerned for the sheep but having a giggle. As we approached the green some 500 yards from the tee there was a ball sitting on the fairway 15 yards from the green. On examination, it was found to be Graham's original ball and he had just completed the longest uphill drive I had ever seen. We collapsed in fits of laughter. I lost touch with Graham about four years after that incident, but at that time he still had the ball appropriately disinfected of course.

MR R MILLER (PERTH, SCOTLAND)

... AND NEVER EAT BEANS ON MATCH DAY

You're the caddy! You try and
remember where you left them.

SHOCKING!

WHILE ON HOLIDAY, my buddy and I discovered a lovely scenic course at Criccieth in Wales. I am an arthritis sufferer so it is with baseball grip that I tee off first on a cold frosty September morning. We reached the green in 3 (managing to avoid free roaming sheep and their droppings) to find a wire fence to keep the sheep off. My partner grudgingly lets me move my ball 6" from the fence. I'm going to sink the 25 ft putt for my first par of the day, when I had the worst attack of cramps in my knuckles that I have ever had. I line up again and wham! - the same thing happens. I'm just about to cry off when I see my mate doubled up with laughter. The fence was electrified.

MR R DONALD (DONCASTER)

AN EXPENSIVE LESSON

A FELLOW WAS on a business trip to Liverpool and took his clubs with him. He decided to play one evening on his own at the local municipal course. On the first tee he sliced the ball wildly out of bounds. At that moment another man was passing, immaculately dressed in Pringle sweater and slacks. He came over and offered encouragement. "Try that again, but this time keep your head still and your eye on the ball until after you've hit it, and slow down your swing." So he did this, and hit the ball beautifully down the middle. After admiring his shot he turned to thank the man, but he was gone along with the businessman's clubs.

MR A CROSS (KIRKELLA)

No, Sly, throwing is cheating.

A SHORTS STORY

FOR THE RECORD I am over 75 years old and play at least one full round every day - quite often two, and have done so for the past 16-17 years. The following are actual happenings.
I had just finished my round of Golf and was wearing shorts and long socks as is permitted. I went into the Men's Bar for a drink when a friend called me from the lounge which was quite full, so I went to him. It is not allowed to wear shorts in the lounge and the Secretary came over and said "You can't wear shorts in here." I looked at him and carried on my conversation with my friend and at the same time took my shorts off. Never had much to show anyway!

MR W D KNIGHT (HATFIELD, HERTS)

Gill's lawyers
will never find
me now.

BOYS WILL BE

THERE WAS A golf course which had a short par 3 hole with a slight dog leg, which although only slight, obscured the green from the tee. Two lads hid in the bushes near the green and waited for the first round to arrive. When both players had teed off and the balls had passed round the dog leg, the lads, knowing they could not be seen nipped out and moved the balls. One they placed on the green about 3 ft from the pin, the other was put in the hole. Then they waited in the bushes for the golfers to arrive. The players reached the green, saw one ball close to the pin, no sight of the other ball. When they checked, the owner of the ball on the green was elated. The other searched for his begrudgingly praising the other's good fortune. After a while the first golfer decided to putt his ball and when his partner went to the flag he saw the ball in the hole, checked it and now it was his turn to be happy, a hole in one. After they had gone and the next victims played, they put one ball on the green and the other under the lip of a nearby bunker. Then watched them play, one birdie, the other struggling to get out of the bunker. They did this on and off all morning and no one realised until back at the clubhouse a pattern emerged. Several holes in one, several birdies and bogies. They must have suspected foul play.

MR A ROWLAND (CHICHESTER)

ENTERPRISING INITIATIVE

AS A YOUNG MAN of 15 I played on a course that had two blind second shots, so if a ball went into the rough this was often not seen by the player concerned and resulted in plenty of balls being lost. I then used to spend time after school and at weekends scouring the rough for these balls and then selling them. This funded my golf; a new bag, putter and numerous drivers. This continued until I reached the age of 18, old enough to drink. Thereafter, my time was spent at the 19th and not searching for balls. It soon became obvious that my income needed to be subsidised and I didn't like the idea of trudging the course searching for balls. I had to think of something that would fund my drinking and save me hunting for lost balls. The solution came quickly. As I have mentioned there were a couple of blind tee shots on the course, one of these a par three, it was easy. Wait in the bushes until a ball arrived on the green, run out, drop the ball in the hole and return to my hiding place. I would do this two or three times before returning to the clubhouse bar awaiting the 'hole in ones' to come in and celebrate with the traditional drink for everyone, keeping my thirst quenched and the 'hole in one' board engraver very busy.

I no longer live in the area but recently visited some friends that live nearby and decided to visit the course again. My tee shot on the said hole sailed over the hill in the direction of the green. When I reached the green my ball was about fourteen feet from the hole (but I still checked the bushes) and when I reached the clubhouse I was not surprised to see the huge reduction in the number of 'holes in one' registered on the board since I'd moved.

MR G TATHAM (BRIGHTON)

HEAVY WORK

ONE OF MY LOCAL PUBS, the Hole in the Wall, has a golf tournament every year for a few of the lads. One Sunday lunchtime we were sat talking about the next one. As I had never played golf before Kev said I could go along and caddy for him. Kev's the pub joker, always setting people up or taking the mickey out of someone. I didn't think anything could happen just caddying for him (how wrong I was). On the day of the tournament we arrived at the golf course and the lads were getting their clubs out of the cars. I asked Kev where his trolley was. "I don't need a trolley, that's what I've got a caddy for," he said. Just before we set off I asked him how he thought he would do? It's in the bag was his confident reply.

Kev wasn't playing very well, but he kept on saying, "Don't worry it's in the bag". By the time we had reached the 6th hole I was getting a bit tired, the golf bag seemed really heavy. None of the other lads that were caddying seemed tired, so I just carried on. When we got to the 13th hole there was a bank up to it. I was struggling a bit by then but the others were walking up with ease, laughing and joking, so I still said nothing. We got round the rest of the course, but every time Kev saw me struggle with the bag he said, "Come on, it's in the bag."

When it was all over we went back to the pub for a few pints and the presentation. After the landlord had presented the winners with their trophies he said they had a special prize for the best caddy. He called my name out and as I went up all the lads cheered and shouted as I was presented with what looked like a case of beer, but when I opened it inside was a very large block of concrete. It was the same block of concrete that had been in the bottom of Kev's golf bag which I had just carried round 18 holes and I got a mug which read, "I'm a mug for golf". It was only then that I realised what he meant when he said, "It's in the bag".

I've taken up the game since and this year I'm going to get my own back and win the tournament.

MR S JOHNSON (CO DURHAM)

And if that doesn't work, just hit the hell out of it.

DOUBLE BLUFF

IN THE MID '50S I was a junior member of the St Deiniol Golf Club in Bangor, North Wales. On Saturdays I used to caddy for one of the senior members of the Club, Mr Breen-Turner. On the Saturday that the story I am about to relate happened Mr Breen-Turner was unable to play golf, so I was walking around the course with a few clubs hoping for a bit of practice. As some of the male members of the club were playing in a friendly match at one of the neighbouring courses St Deiniol was very quiet. This meant that the lady members who were normally not allowed to play the course before 3 pm on Saturdays could play earlier. On the day in question I was standing on a rock by the third, a short par 3, watching a ladies four ball tee off. One of the ladies tee shots finished about 2 inches from the hole although they would not know this from where they were standing as they would only see the top of the flag. Fortunately I did not mention to the lady how close her ball was to the hole.

The ladies were making their way from the tee to the green which was separated by quite a steep gully I was still standing on the rock which was a good vantage point when I saw one of two male golfers who had just teed off from the fourth tee run onto the third green and tap the ball into the hole. When the ladies arrived on the green and found that the ball was in the hole you can imagine their reaction. The screams of joy and laughter filled the air, while the two male members standing around the corner enjoyed their little joke, not knowing their prank had been witnessed.

The punch line to this story is that on the day before (Friday) this same lady member had a genuine hole in one on the same hole.

H ROBERTS (CO DURHAM)

EXHIBITION PLAY

IT WAS A SUNNY evening when we teed off for our usual Wednesday three ball. By the time we had reached the 9th hole, Simon, John and myself, we had all given up on a good score. We decided that we would just enjoy ourselves and have a bit of fun. Simon said to me, being the joker of the pack, "why don't you try playing your tee shot while kneeling down?" Simon had seen this done by Sevy in an exhibition. Anyway, I got in position and took a big swing.

To our astonishment the ball flew about 180 yards onto the front of the green. On our way to the next par 3, the 12th, we had a good laugh at my golfing feat. The 12th, being very similar to the 9th in distance, is more difficult because of the long carry over Mini Valley. I decided to use the same club, a 3 wood. The ball was teed a little higher this time to try and get that extra bit of carry and distance I needed to clear the valley. Once again I knelt down and swung the club. It was a good shot again. John said, "That's on the green". It pitched on the front of the green and began to roll towards the hole. We all thought it but nobody said it until Simon said, "It's going in the hole". In disbelief we watched as it fell softly into the hole for an unbelievable ace.

The next day after the news of my miracle shot had filtered around the club I was called to the manager's office. Firstly for a good ticking off about messing about on the course. I was told to keep my trick shots to the practice area. Secondly to arrange a time for the local press, who had also heard about my shot, to come and take a photo and make a report for the local newspaper, the Tenby Observer. They came to do an article which appeared in the next issue. This all added to an unbelievable week in my life.

MR G SCOTCHER (PEMBROKESHIRE)

LOST AND FOUND

JUST RECENTLY TWO new members joined our golf club, husband and wife who take their dog around with them. On this particular day they went round the course as usual. On the fourth fairway the woman hit her ball into the woods which runs alongside the course. She went in to look for her ball while her husband waited on the fairway with the dog. She went through the woods after losing her way and down a road into a village about a mile away. Here she phoned for a taxi and asked the driver to take her to the golf club where she asked someone to lend her some money to pay the fare. When she got into the club she saw the secretary and asked him if he had seen her husband. He said he hadn't, so she walked up the fourth fairway looking for him and there he was, exactly where she had left him with the dog. When he saw her he said, "Did you find it?"

MR D SMART (E SUSSEX)

LEE TREVINO TOP TEN

1 I'm hitting the driver so good, I gotta dial the operator for long distance after I hit it.

2 They say I'm famous for my delicate chip shots. Sure, when I hit 'em right, they land, just so, like a butterfly with sore feet.

3 There are two things that don't last long – dogs that chase cars and pros that putt for pars.

4 If my IQ had been two points lower, I'd have been a plant somewhere.

5 In lightning, hold up a one-iron and walk. Even God can't hit a one-iron.

6 You can make a lot of money in this game. Just ask my ex-wives. Both of them are so rich that neither of their husbands work.

7 No one who ever had lessons would have a swing like mine.

 8 When J.C.Sneed was a kid, he was so ugly, they had to tie a pork chop around his neck to get the dog to play with him.

 9 I can't wait to wake up in the morning to hear what I have to say!

 10 Show me someone who gets angry once in a while, and I'll show you a guy with a killer instinct. Show me a guy walking down the fairway smiling and I'll show you a loser.

CLIFF HANGER

A GOLFER watched in amazement as a ball he had driven over a sheer cliff face was lobbed back to him by a rock climber. John Cooper of Bayston Hill, Shrewsbury, said it happened as he enjoyed a day out with three fellow golfers at Llanymynech golf course. He said: "I was playing in a four ball and was coming down the 18th when I put the ball over the cliff. I was just walking away to play another shot when I saw this climber coming over the top of the cliff. He had scaled the 150 foot cliff just to throw my ball back to me. It was the talk of the green."

MR J COOPER (SHREWSBURY)

❛ Some people pay women with whips and manacles to inflict pain on them — others play golf. ❜

In golf the ball usually lies poorly, but the player well.

Listen Mark, I'll try anything if it improves my swing.

Look like a woman, but play like a man.

JAN STEPHENSON

I may not be the prettiest girl in the world, but I'd like to see Bo Derek rate a '10' after playing 18 holes in 100-degree heat.

JAN STEPHENSON

> ' Maybe people will stop thinking of me only as a sex symbol and realise i can really play golf. '
>
> **JAN STEPEHENSON**

6 The pleasure derived from hitting the ball dead centre on the club is comparable only to one or two other pleasures that come to mind at the moment. 9

DINAH SHORE

Golf humanises women, humbles their haughty natures, tends, in short, to knock out of their systems a certain modicum of the superciliousness, that swank, which makes wooing a tough proposition for the diffident male.

P G WODEHOUSE

6 Women who seek equality with men lack ambition. 9

PATTY SHEEHAN
BUMPER STICKER

First Man: 'I just got a new set of clubs for my wife.'
Second Man : 'Now that's what I call a real good trade.'

6 Just ask yourself how good Nicklaus would be if he had to do his nails and put up hair every night before a tournament? Could he shoot sixty-eight if he was trying to make up his mind which dress to wear to the party that night? 9

JIM MURRAY

His handicap was down to twelve. But these things are not all. A golfer needs a loving wife, to whom he can describe the day's play through the long evenings.

P G WODEHOUSE

6 He quit playing when i started outdriving him. 9

JOANNE CARNER
ON HER HUSBAND

6 if ah didn't have these ah'd hit it twenty yards further. 9

BABE DIDRIKSON
ZAHARIAS,
ON HER BREASTS

‘ i remember being upset once and telling my Dad i wasn't following through right, and he replied, 'Nancy, it doesn't make any difference to a ball what you do after you hit it. ’

NANCY LOPEZ

Where will you be going on your holidays next year, Doris?

OVER THE LIMIT UNDERWRITERS

THE HOST WAS delighted at the success of the day so far. The venue, Chestfield Golf Club was set in the heart of the garden of England and sported the oldest custom built clubhouse in England. The morning round had been played in bright sunshine with just a balmy breeze to cool the brow. Lunch had been sumptuous and complimented by a more than ample supply of Puligny Montrachet followed by Havanas and Taylors vintage port. It was after lunch that the host realised he had made one organisational error. The first two in from the morning were the last two out on the afternoon and the port had remained stationary in front of them for two hours. The two were leading underwriters from Lloyds of London and had enthusiastically taken their fill of the refreshments on offer. As they swayed on the tee, waiting for the fairway to clear, two more visitors arrived, accompanied by caddies.

The new arrivals were obviously semi-professionals as they were wearing Armani polo shirts and shiny Ping clubs peeped from their bags. To the host's horror they began to converse in German. The fairway was now clear and the first underwriter stepped onto the tee. He took an enormous swing. The heel of his club connected with the equator of the ball. It shot forward, reaching a height of three inches. Just before it attained the speed of sound it met the ladies tee box, shot fifty feet into the air and in gentle parabola, found its way back to the front of the tee from where it had commenced its brief journey. The German visitors appeared less than amused and "Mein Gott, nein verr gut mit der hitten shtick" was heard.

The second underwriter strode on to the tee chuckling at his partner's embarrassment. He placed his ball and swung as though he was flogging a galley slave. At least four inches of daylight was visible as the club head passed the stationary ball. The underwriter peered into the distance trying to see where the ball had disappeared. Eventually he looked down and saw his own ball standing proudly atop the tee peg and his partner's three feet in front. He stepped back, bowed graciously to the waiting pair and said, "Would you like to play through?"

MR J LAVERS (KENT)

❛ if you drink, dont drive. Don't even putt. ❜

DEAN MARTIN

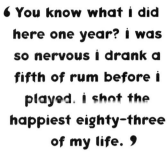

6 You know what i did here one year? i was so nervous i drank a fifth of rum before i played. i shot the happiest eighty-three of my life. 9

CHI CHI RODRIGUEZ

Two Wood Or Not Two Wood

THE HEAVENS WERE crying for all the souls who had lost their balls. The course unplayable. The steward, an enterprising man, opened the nineteenth so the waiting throng could while away the time until the weather relented. The Captain, as a leader of men, was first to the bar. At twelve the course reopened. The Captain meandered like a river towards the first, followed by the senior caddy. After several attempts the Captain managed to insert his tee in the ground and balance a Pinnacle atop it. He turned to the caddy and cried, "Gi'us the two wood". The caddy produced it and placed it in his hand.

He stood closing alternate eyes in a vain attempt to reduce the number of balls in his vision. Eventually he had got them down to three and elected to aim for the middle one. He lashed at the ball, throwing himself four paces forward to the front of the tee. To the surprise of everyone, including the caddy, the ball flew straight and true for two hundred and sixty yards and settled in the middle of the fairway. The caddy looked to heaven, knowing that God had just smiled on his master. He replaced the two wood in the bag, produced a wedge and dutifully followed the Captain as he staggered up the fairway. On reaching the ball the Captain studied it intently. He turned to the caddy who was proffering the wedge and said, "Gi'us the two wood". The caddy

protested that the distance was only fifty yards and maybe the wedge would be a better choice. "I'm playing thish game not you," the Captain proclaimed.

After two minutes of the alternating eyes routine the Captain lunged at the innocent ball. The club struck the ground at least six inches behind the ball and dug in like a JCB. The divot was driven up at such a rate that it propelled the ball. It leaped forward and meandered onto the green, eventually stopping two inches from the hole. The caddy looked up expecting the sky to open and a voice say, "This is my son in whom I am well pleased." The caddy walked onto the green, putter in hand, to be confronted with, "Gi'us the two wood." After the previous contretemps the caddy decided that obedience was better than conflict and produced the two wood. The Captain swayed over the ball and the club head surged downwards and past the ball without making contact. The draught, caused by the passing wood, was just enough to blow the ball into the hole. The caddy did not look skywards as he now knew that he was actually caddying for his maker. The Captain fell to his knees and peered at the ball nestling in the cup. After several minutes studying the situation, he stood, turned to the caddy and said, "Bloody awful lie, gi'us the sand iron."

MR J LAVERS (KENT)

European Ryder Cup Victory 1995 in USA. The Duke of York rang through to congratulate the players.

'Sam, can you take this call, it's the Duke of York.'

'Tell them i'll settle my slate when i get back.'

THEY SAY THAT golf is the sport of busy men - and 13 of the last 16 American presidents have proved the point by reaching for their clubs when they need a break from global power-broking.

President Wilson played 18 holes before declaring war on Germany in 1917 - and Eisenhower was dragged off the course when the American U2 spy plane was shot down by the Soviets in 1960.

RUSTLING UP A fourball is slightly more complex for world leaders than for the average follower of the game.

When President Clinton decided to drop in on the Orinda Country Club near San Francisco, the delighted course official's were suddenly swamped by men sporting earpieces, macs and dark glasses.

Secret service agents checked the course and set up a communications net, then ran security probes on all the clubhouse staff. They demanded 17 buggies - two for Clinton and his playing partners, and 15 for the bodyguards.

The men's changing rooms were cleared, all bags were put through an x-ray machine, and even the balls, tees, and a towel from the pro shop were screened.

Two marksmen with sniper rifles followed the play from trees on either side of the course and a helicopter was on standby.

And after all that preparation, Clinton forgot his shoes, and the pro shop had none in his size!

> **6 if i had my way, any man guilty of golf would be ineligible for any office of trust in the United States 9**
>
> HENRY L. MENCKEN

PRESIDENTIAL GOLFING days have brought some famous incidents. Richard Nixon was once caught throwing his ball out of a bush and Bill Clinton, who plays off 20, is unapologetic about taking literally dozens of mulligans on a round.

President Kennedy, a fine player with a 7 handicap, was notorious for pointing out hazards on the course - while his opponent was on the back swing.

LYNDON JOHNSON once warned a junior on the course, "One lesson you'd better learn if you want to be in politics is that you never go out on a golf course and beat the President."

And 'Gimmes' awarded to Presidential golfers are some of the biggest in the game. But it all stops when the term of office comes to an end. Soon after leaving the White House he noticed: "I find I no longer win every golf game I play."

> 6 i know i'm getting better at golf because i'm hitting fewer spectators. 9
>
> GERALD R FORD

> 6 He doesn't know he can't hit the ball through the trunk of a tree. 9
>
> JACK NICKLAUS ON FORD

Gerald Ford, here looking appropriately like the Grim Reaper, was the President who brought real danger into the game of golf.

Although he once played off 12, his wayward game caused carnage among spectators, and partners demanded bravery medals for going out with him.

It's not hard to find Jerry Ford on a golf course, you just follow the wounded.

BOB HOPE

Jerry Ford has made golf a contact sport.

BOB HOPE

Jerry Ford – the most dangerous driver since Ben Hur.

BOB HOPE

President Ford waits until he hits his first drive to know what course he's playing that day.

BOB HOPE

Ex-Vice President Dan Quayle, despite his style, is a high calibre golfer who caught the bug in a big way.

His Wife Marilyn sighed:"Dan would rather play golf than have sex any day".

PURE GENIE-US

AN ELDERLY HUSBAND and his pretty young wife were enjoying their round of golf when they came to the tricky sixteenth dog-leg, which was just over four hundred yards. He looked down the fairway and at the trees which bordered it, had a few practice swings, turned to aim at the trees and the ball soared in the direction of the green. Before he had a chance to relish his shot he heard a tremendous crash of glass. When he finally got through the trees he saw an enormous man, wonderfully built and as handsome as the devil, standing near a greenside bunker.

"Did you see my ball?" the husband asked.

"See it, your ball just smashed that big bottle in the bunker," the man replied.

"I'm sorry if I surprised you," said the husband.

"I'm not, I've been in that bottle for at least three hundred years and now your ball has released me. My most grateful thanks."

"I hope you're not hurt," said the husband. The man shook his head and said "I wish to repay you for your act of kindness. Ask for any three wishes and I will grant them."

"You want to give me three wishes?" asked the husband. "Anything you wish."

"Right, well let me see, yes I know, I'd like to be able to drive a golf ball three hundred yards if I have to."

"You've got your wish."

"And every shot I hit onto a green must finish no more than ten feet from the hole."

"It is yours".

"And every putt I make drops into the hole."

"Granted. Now having released me from that miserable bottle, I'd like you to do something for me."

"If I can, certainly," said the husband.

"Well, it's been so long since I've known the pleasure a beautiful woman can give, I wonder if you would allow me to spend the next hour or so with your companion?"

"Are you mad?" asked the husband.

"Are you mad?" replied the woman. "You have just become the greatest golfer the world has ever seen and you are about to quibble about an hour of my time. Anyway it's a small sacrifice to make it if helps you darling."

"All right," said the husband, "one hour."

With that the blonde, bronzed 'Adonis' approached the woman, bowed and led her gently in the direction of the woods. "Tell me, how old is your husband?" he asked.

"He's sixty," said the young woman.

"That's a bit old to believe in genies isn't it?"

MR R BIRD (CHESHIRE)

MOTHER KNOWS BEST

A GOLFER WHO was a mad, green conservationist sliced his ball into a patch of buttercups. Such was his love for all things flora he picked out his ball and penalised himself the statutory one shot. At that moment there appeared from behind the nearest tree a little old lady dressed totally in green who said, "I am Mother Nature and for your consideration to those defenceless flowers you will be rewarded with free butter for the rest of your life." "Thank you very much," answered the golfer, "but where the hell were you when I was trapped under the pussy willow tree."

MR W DAVIDSON (CAMBRIDGE)

And when you make it to the top, your sponsors always treat you with dignity.

> **❝ Golf is a game where white men can dress up as black pimps and get away with it. ❞**
>
> ROBIN WILLIAMS

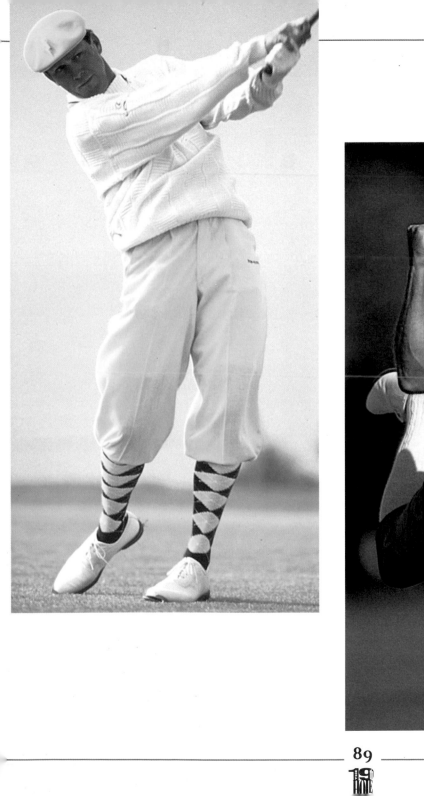

SCOTLAND THE BRAVE

HAMISH AND BRUCE were two crofters who managed their own smallholdings in a sparsely populated area of the Scottish Highlands. Both were married with fairly large families but still managed to break free from the shackles of their extremely hard working lives on most Sundays to hack their way round the nearby golf course, which although tended by two competent greenkeepers still abounded with gorse and heather strewn rocky rough.

Both were having their normal Sunday round on a bleak, blustery and snowy November afternoon. After slogging round the course, both failing in their attempt to break 100 for the first time they trudged wearily into the clubhouse stiff with cold, ordered two large whiskies and sat down with snow encrusted beards at a corner table in the nearby empty lounge.

After several glasses of whisky and an hour and a half of thawing out, during which time hardly a word had passed between them, Hamish suddenly said, "Well, same time next week Bruce?" To which Bruce replied "Aye - weather permittin'."

MR S STEPHEN (EDINBURGH)

WATER EVERYWHERE, NOT A DROP TO DRINK

AN AMERICAN was playing St Andrews with a scottish caddy in the pouring rain and after every shot he took a swig of Whisky from his hip flask without offering the caddy a drink. Finally in frustration he shouted: "God almighty isn't there one dry place on this goddam island?" The caddy replied, "You could try the back of my throat."

MR F HAGAN (LYTHAM-ST-ANNES)

The difference between a sand trap and water is the difference between a car crash and an airplane crash. You have a chance of recovering from a car crash.

BOBBY JONES

LIGHTNING REACTIONS

AT OUR LAST golf society match of the year, we were playing at Alresford Golf Club, where the main prize for the match winner is a St. Andrews hickory shaft putter, mounted on a presentation plaque. This was to be the venue where I had set myself the goal of winning this much sought after prize. My playing partners were Sean Kennedy (24) and Steve Batten (18), while I was playing off of 22. It was a dark humid cloudy day and the golf wasn't much better. I was spraying the ball to all parts of the course, and although I was picking up points regularly I knew that it wouldn't be enough to win. What I needed was some divine intervention, and although I didn't know it at the time, I was going to get it!

It then started to rain with large drops as big as a golf hole, until it proceeded to come down like Niagara Falls. "Here we go" I thought, taking my glasses off to wipe them, "things can't get worse, I can't see now!" Things did get worse.

So all three of us fumbled about pulling on our waterproofs and manfully carried on. We then heard the first deep rumbles of thunder, "God", I though, "first rain now thunder. Things can't get worse".

Yes they did. I said to the lads that I was worried about carrying on with lightning about, when you hear all these stories of golfers being hit. Sean then said, "Don't worry lads, I'm a bit of an expert when it comes to lightning as I've been hit twice before." "Oh no" I thought I'm playing golf in a thunderstorm, with a guy who thinks he's a lightning conductor".

Sean then gave us the benefit of his expert advice by counting the interval between the flashes and the rumbles of thunder. No problem he said counting to twenty, it's 5 miles away. By this time we were on the tenth green. The next count was fifteen but our resident meteorological expert was confident in the lightning passing us by and so we raised our brollies checked our waterproofs and waded onwards. The course was flooding by this time. The tenth green was nearly a wash out. Putting was a watery lottery. We had a quick meeting and decided on the basis of our resident weather expert and his estimation of the whereabouts of the lighting we would go on to the eleventh tee.

There was then a huge bang, like an explosion, as an oak tree close to the nearby ninth green was struck by a lightning bolt. The lightning then shot across to the tee where we were standing throwing us to the ground like nine pins. I shouted at Sean with my ears still ringing from the thunder, "I thought you said it was miles away". Sean replied, "Sorry, I've been struggling with my yardage all day".

MR C FULLER (ALTON)

A TIGHT FIT

AFTER REGULARLY complaining about the cold weather during the winter months a friend of mine was told he should put on a pair of his old lady's tights to keep him warm while playing golf. Thinking it was a great idea he decided to give it a go. He turned up the following Sunday as planned to play our regular fourball and while parking the car mouthed to us that he'd tried as he was told. He got out of the car with ladies tights on, over his trousers and jacket, complete with golf shoes and holes in his knees where he'd had trouble getting them on. "I don't think much to this idea," he said. "It would have been better if you'd have put them on under your trousers don't you think?" we replied. He wondered why everyone was rolling about the floor laughing.

MR B JONES (MILTON KEYNES)

'The player may experiment about his swing, his grip, his stance. it is only when he begins asking his caddy's advice that he is getting on dangerous ground. '

SIR WALTER SIMPSON

BIG SHOW OFF

JESUS SAYS to his father, "Dad, let's have a game of golf. It's Sunday and everyone's at Church so it will be OK." "Right," says God, "off you go." Jesus hits a tee shot 300 yards down the middle of the fairway. God takes his shot which goes into the trees. A squirrel sees the ball and picks it up and runs across the fairway. An eagle sees the squirrel, swoops down, snatches it up and flies off. A black cloud appears over the eagle and a lightning bolt hits the eagle on the back of the head. He drops the squirrel and it lands on the edge of the green, the ball rolls out of his mouth, across the green into the hole. Jesus says, "Are you going to keep messing about or are you going to play golf?"

MR D WEBSTER (HERTS)

ADVANCE BOOKINGS

A GOLFER WHOSE long term partner had died consulted a psychic in the hope of a message. "Good news and bad," was the answer. "Your friend says he has already played a beautiful course in Heaven, unfortunately you will be teeing off with him at 10 am tomorrow."

it's no use Seve, the PGA won't accept Masons.

MISSED AGAIN

A VICAR AND his partner were on the 16th when the partner missed an easy putt.

Partner: "God dammit, I've missed."

Vicar: "Please don't swear in my presence."

At the 17th the partner fails to sink another sitter.

Partner: "God dammit, I've missed again."

Vicar: "Don't you realise that God could strike you dead for taking his name in vain?"

At the 18th once again the partner fails to sink a simple tap in.

Partner: "God dammit, I've missed again." Suddenly there's a clap of thunder and a bolt of lightning hits the 18th green. When the smoke clears, the vicar lies dead and a voice from the clouds says.

"God dammit, I've missed again."

MR P CONNEELY (AYLESBURY, BUCKS)

I told ya Greg. God don't like jokes about Jack Nicklaus.

GOD'S LAW

A MAN WENT to see his priest and said to him, "Father, I have sinned, I blasphemed while I was out playing golf." "What happened?" asked the priest. "Well," said the man, "I teed off on a par 5 and hit my drive well but it faded at the last minute and went into the trees." "Was this when you blasphemed?" asked the priest. "No" said the man, "I had a good lie and was able to hit the ball with my 5 wood, it scorched off a treat, but faded again at the last minute and landed in a greenside bunker." "Was this when you blasphemed?" asked the priest. "No," said the man, "I managed a good chip out of the bunker and the ball stopped just 2 feet from the hole." "Don't tell me," said the priest groaning, "you missed the God damned putt!"

MR B BAKER (PINNER)

THE NON-PRACTISING PREACHER

A VICAR RENOWNED for his sermons against the evils of breaking the Sabbath and doing anything on the Lord's day, decides one Sunday afternoon to play golf on a rare day off. Looking down St Peter says to his boss, "Have you seen him? The hypocrite not practising what he preaches." "Yes" says God, "I think I will punish him." On the next tee shot on a 365 yard par 4 the vicar takes his shot and watches the ball fly straight down the fairway across the green and into the cup for a magnificent hole in one. "Hang on," said St Peter. "I thought you were going to punish him." "I have," said God, "who can he tell?"

MR D WEBSTER (HERTS)

> **6 Golf is a game in which you are alone with your creator. 9**
>
> ANGUS MacVICAR

ADVICE FROM THE TOP

A CHAP GOES to his local course to play a round of golf but there is no-one to play with so he goes out alone. He hits the sweetest drive ever up the first, splitting the fairway, lawns his second and holes the putt for a birdie. The same thing on the second, but just misses the 30 foot putt and taps in for par. After fifteen holes of playing the best golf of his life he is 3 under gross as he walks onto the sixteenth tee. Unfortunately this has always been his bogey hole. A par three across water and the best score he has ever achieved is a seven, so he stands on the tee and thinks 'Dear God, whilst I have never been a religious man I have always tried to be a good man. I have never asked for anything before, but please just this once let me hit the green for one.'

At this a voice booms out from a small cloud and says 'take a seven iron out,' which he does. Then the voice says 'use a blue castle tee,' which he does. Then the voice says 'now take out a Titleist 100' and as he opens the box to do so the voice says, 'Not a new one you idiot!'

MR G REES (HERTS)

A Much Imp-roved Game

A GOLFER OUT having a round on his own one day, hit an awful drive and set off in search of his wayward ball. On finding his ball set awkwardly in a hollow, he ponders on how best to play the shot when he spots a leprechaun sat on a tree stump laughing his head off.

"Call yourself a golfer?" cried the imp. "How would you like to improve and play like a true professional?" Thinking about it the golfer asked what the catch was. "Only a small one," said the imp. "But you have to agree first before you find out what it is". "OK" said the golfer, "I'm fed up of playing like a true hacker. I accept, now what's the forfeit?" "You will find your sex life is less than what it used to be," cried the imp, then disappeared.

Years later having won every title going, he was back at his old course giving a demonstration, when he struck a wayward shot. Off he went to seek his ball when a familiar voice from the bushes asked how his golf was going on. Spotting the imp, the golfer replied, "Fantastic. I've won every major tournament. I can't do a thing wrong and it's all down to you. I can't thank you enough." Shocked at the reply the imp asked, "But have you suffered with your love life?" "Not much." replied the golfer, "I still manage to get it once a month and for a village priest that's not bad."

MR B GILL (WORCESTER)

Some Fathers Do 'Ave Em

IN SCOTLAND every year the priests play the ministers at golf. For the past 20 years the priests have always won. The moderator of the Church of Scotland phoned the Captain of the Ministers and told him he was a friend of Sam Torrance and if he would put him in a dog collar they would have a chance of beating the priests this year. On the evening after the game the moderator phoned the Captain to ask how they fared.

Captain:	Beaten again.
Moderator:	How did Sam Torrance do?
Captain:	He got well cuffed.
Moderator:	Who beat him?
Captain	Some Father Ballersteros.

MR J O'HARA (BLACKPOOL)

Holy Water

JESUS CHRIST came down to earth to play Augusta with Peter as his caddy. As Jesus played a lovely drive at the 15th, laying up just short of the water 120 yards to the green he turned to Peter and said "pass me the wedge". Peter said, "you'll never reach with a wedge you need your 9 iron". Jesus said, "pass me the wedge". Peter said, "You'll never reach". Jesus said, "last year in the Masters, Jack Nicklaus was in this exact spot and hit a wedge 6" from the pin." Dutifully Peter handed him the wedge and sure enough the ball was short and landed in the water. Jesus then walked on the water to retrieve his ball. A passing golfer shouted to Peter, "Who does he think he is Jesus Christ". Peter replied, "No Jack Nicklaus."

MR C WOODFIELD (BIRMINGHAM)

Ten bucks says you can't hit the one in the red bikini.

SEX, LIES AND GOLF COURSES

COURSE HUMOUR

AFTER PLAYING a round of golf with three pals we were in the clubhouse enjoying a drink. John said he had to leave as the only way he could play that day was by promising to take his wife out and buy her a new dress. Alan turned to him and commented that he too had to leave to decorate the lounge. Maurice turned to them and said they had got off lightly as the only way he could get out to play was by promising to take his wife to Florida and he had to leave to organise the trip. Before the three of them left, John remarked that I never had any problems to get out and play golf and asked how I did it. I said, "I woke up this morning, turned to my wife and said golf course or intercourse? and she replied, 'Don't forget your sweater.'"

MR D SEARSON (BRISTOL)

THE LUCKY LEPRECHAUN

A 24 HANDICAP GOLFER was playing at Ballybunion golf course in Ireland and he's hitting the ball all over the course. After finally hitting his 14th shot at a par 4 and still not reaching the green, he dumps his clubs in a hollow tree and starts walking away.

Suddenly a little voice calls out, "I am a lucky leprechaun, I will grant you three wishes for releasing me from the spell of the hollow tree. I know your wife is a poor golfer and spends all your money but I must warn you that any wish you request your wife will get to a greater extent. What is your first wish?"

"I would like to be a 4 handicap came the reply."

"Your wish is granted, but your wife will play off 1. What is your second wish?"

"I would like £250,000 put in our joint bank account."

"Your wish is granted, but your wife will have £750,000. What is your third and final wish?"

After some thought the golfer replied, "Can I have a mild heart attack?"

MR G PARKER (WATFORD)

BARKING MAD

A GOLF ADDICT turns to his frigid wife and says, "Tomorrow you and I are going to watch Nick Faldo at the Open. We'll take the dog too." "No way," she replied. "It's either that or we have an orgy," he threatens. She'd rather put up with the sex. On stripping his clothes off, she sees he is covered with bites and scratches. "OK, so the dog hates golf too."

MR D RITCHIE (HERTS)

SIZE ISN'T IMPORTANT

PLAYING GOLF WITH a male friend, my wife decided to join us for game. Whilst playing the 17th hole a par 3 uphill hole about 165 yards with a raised plateau green, my wife left her tee shot well short, leaving a very tricky pitch. Much to my surprise she played a lovely second shot, the ball stopping about 8 inches away. As she could not see it she asked how close it was and trying to be rather boastful in front of my friend I replied, "Good shot, it's about the length of my willy away". To which my wife promptly replied, "Just leave it, it might fall in the hole."

MR G WOOD (LIVINGSTON)

A DIFFICUILT HOLE

A GIRL WHO ONLY dated Golf Pros was chatted up by a local golf shop pro.

"Well," said the girl "I'm used to real pros."

"I am a real pro," said the lad.

"But my last boyfriend was Seve Ballesteros," said the girl, "but I'll go to dinner with you".

Following dinner and some wine they found themselves in a hotel bed. After a rigorous bout of lovemaking the young pro went to get up.

"Where are you going?" said the girl.

"To the shower," came the reply.

"Seve would not do that," she said.

"What would Seve do?" he asked.

"Well, he would call room service, have them send up Champagne and we would drink and make love again."

"OK," said the pro, "that's what we'll do."

He called room service, they drank the Champagne and made love again. The pro then went to get out of bed.

"Where are you going?" she asked again, and received the same reply.

"Seve wouldn't do that," she said again.

"What would he do this time?" asked the pro.

He got the same reply.

"OK," he said again. "Room Service, a bottle of Champagne please." After another bout of drinking and lovemaking he again started to leave the bed only to be stopped with the same retort.

"Look," said the pro, "have you got Seve's number?"

"Why?' she asked.

"I would like to find out what the par is for this hole," he replied.

MR D WEBSTER (HERTS)

I'll Show You Mine...

ONE UNFORGETTABLE day last summer everything that could have gone wrong did. That day my luck started off bad and rapidly deteriorated. Slamming the betting shop door, having backed 25 consecutive losers, I made my way to the car only to find it clamped. An hour later and £60 poorer, having kicked a pocketful of the bookie's pens into orbit, I decided upon a round of golf to ease my shattered nerves. A strange face at my club volunteered to give me a game adding that he was very wary because I had a lucky face. Three hours later with him having won every hole, I remarked that looks were often deceptive as I mused at my well depleted wallet. Now down to my last tenner, I was nevertheless determined to strike one winning bet, before heading home. My trump card was the fact that I had been born with three testicles. "Bet you my last ten pounds that we've got five testicles between us." I casually said to the shark. He was very reluctant to accept the wager but after a lot of persuading the bet was struck and he released his belt, dropped his pants and said, "Here's my one, show me your four."

MR P GOLDSMITH (ENFIELD, MIDDX)

A RIGHT HANDER

A MARRIED COUPLE were having a morbid conversation one day and the wife said to her husband, "If I die before you, I've no objection to you finding a new girlfriend." To which he replied, "That's very kind of you dear". "Oh," she said, "I'll go further than that, you can also give her my jewellery."

"That is indeed kind," he said, "I know how much that jewellery means to you."

She said, "I'll go further than that, you can also give her my golf clubs."

"Sorry dear," he said, "I can't do that she's left handed."

MR G DOUGHTY (NORFOLK)

THUMBS UP

THE PRO HAD been giving a female pupil lessons and decided to take her to the main course for a few holes. Standing on the first tee he noticed a couple preparing to take their second shots. "You can drive now," he said thinking there was no way she could reach the other players but she struck a blinder. "Fore" he screamed. One of the other golfers turned then cried out in pain holding his hands between his legs. The worried novice ran down the fairway to the injured male, unzipped his trousers and gave the area a big kiss. "There it's better now isn't it?" she asked. "Yes, but I bet I'll lose the thumbnail" was the reply.

FAIRWAY AFFAIRS

TWO FRIENDS were playing golf one day and playing in front of them were two ladies who were playing very very slowly. One man was getting very hot under the collar and he said to his friend, "Look you're on the Committee, go and ask those ladies to call us through." "I can't do that," his friend replied, "you see the lady on the right is my wife and the one on the left is my bit on the side." In that case then said the other one, "I'll go and tell them," and off he went. When he was about fifty yards from the ladies he turned around and came back. On reaching his friend he said, "Isn't it a small world".

MR G DOUGHTY (NORFOLK)

> ❛ i've had sex in alot of places. i wouldn't want to have it in a bunker, because of the sand. i'd kind of like to have it on the green; it would be nice and soft. ❜
>
> JAN STEPHENSON

THE ODD COUPLE

THIS IS A STORY about an American couple who had just got married. They had only known each other for about four weeks. He was a golf fanatic, she was beautiful and had just put on her negligee and was in bed waiting. "Honey, did I tell you about that game of golf I had last week. It was a great course and I played some good shots. I hit a beautiful drive off the first tee. It must have been 300 yards, only had to chip it to the pin and sank the putt for a birdie. At the second hole I nearly had an ace. It was a perfect shot but I had an unlucky bounce, still I putted for a two, two birdies in a row." His bride yawned. "The third hole, it's a dog leg and I bent that drive beautifully." She yawned again. "Oh, I'm sorry honey, you never did say what you did before we got married." She looked at him. "I used to be a hooker".

"Is that right honey, well I shouldn't worry about it, if you stand square to the ball, keep your right elbow in and swing the club like this....."

MR M CASEY (WILTS)

SAVING ON WASTE

TWO MEN WERE paired for the first time in a golf match. Half way round one asked his partner why he had an attache case fitted to his trolley.

"I'm an assassin, a hit man for the mafia. I have the tools of my trade in the bag which I carry at all times."

"Go on then," his partner replied, "show me". Undoing his case, he assembled the gun and handed it to him. "This is terrific, I can see the far end of the course through these sights, I can even see my house! I can see the windows, look there's my wife in the bedroom. Hang on, she's got a man in there! How much do you charge?" he asked.

"It's £1,000 per bullet," was the reply. "Alright, waste both of them!" The assassin lined up his shot, the rifle going up and down. Then it moved from side to side.

"Come on," said the man, "Do it".

"Hold on," the assassin replied, "I can save you a thousand quid here."

MR D MILLER (NOTTINGHAM)

PLAYING BY THE RULES

RULES OF THE CLUB

Since the admission of women to the club - members are asked to adhere to the following rules:-

Ladies are prohibited from touching gentlemen's balls, either with hands or with clubs.

All holes must be kept clean.

Players are requested to remain silent during short strokes.

All partners must go off together.

When the lady partner goes off first, the gentleman must not delay his strokes but continue to play.

In cases where a lay is impossible, the player may use a new position.

Players deciding on a new lay must start at least a club's length from the hole.

Members are requested to stay out of any hole showing signs of recent repairs - until the red flag has been lifted.

Members are also urged to use reasonable precautions at all times, as the Management cannot be held responsible for balls lost in the brush around the holes.

MRS B MIDGLEY (CLEVELAND)

THE TALE OF TOM, DICK AND HARRY

TOM, DICK AND HARRY are on the first tee. Tom drives off straight up the middle, Dick drives off right into the meadow, Harry drives off into the rough. Dick disappears into the meadow to look for his ball, ten minutes pass by. Harry shouts 'Tom, I'll go and see where Harry is'. Ten minutes pass, so Tom too disappears into the meadow, where he discovers Harry rogering Dick. For Christ's sake, Harry said Tom, you're supposed to be helping him look for his ball. I know said Harry but when I got into the meadow Dick was slumped on the ground, I thought he'd had a heart attack. You're supposed to give him the bloody kiss of life said Tom. Yes, I know, that's how it all started.

MR S DEEMING (BEDWORTH, WARWICKSHIRE)

TOILET HUMOUR

CAUGHT SHORT

DURING A COMPETITION at Dudley golf club, West Midlands, we were playing the monthly medal with players in groups of threes, it was during the round of golf that the following incident occurred. While playing the 15th hole, which unfortunately happens to be one of the furthest from the clubhouse, one of our trio was taken short and was so desperate he could not wait until we had completed our match to use the toilet. He disappeared into the trees and undergrowth, which runs alongside the fairway with his handful of tissues and a pained expression on his face. After approximately three minutes, a much relieved man appeared, to which I promptly informed him that he had incurred a two stroke penalty because it was wiping and placing on fairways only.

MR P ROCK (WEST MIDLANDS)

DUMPED ON

AN OLD FRIEND of mine was playing on our local golf course when he was taken short and had to make use of some nearby bushes. Unfortunately for it a large frog was the recipient of his deposit which rapidly hopped off in disgust. On seeing the laden vehicle he remarked with a scowl, "I've been a member of the town council for fourteen years and this is the first time I've had a motion carried."

MR H BREWIS (CAMBRIDGESHIRE)

PSSSSSS OFF

BERT IS PLAYING golf at his local course and is just about to play his second shot at the 10th hole when he hears, "Pssssssss, pssssssssss!" Bert looks round and sees a bloke in the bushes with his legs apart and his trousers and pants down.

Bloke: "Sorry to disturb you I have been taken short, and just had to go in these bushes, I was desperate I couldn't wait until the clubhouse. Have you got any tissues?"

Bert: "No, sorry I haven't. Bert gets ready to play his shot."

Bloke: "PSSSSSSSS! Have you got a golf towel. I will buy it off you for a fiver, I'm desperate."

Bert: "No I have not got a golf towel."

By now Bert is annoyed and gets ready once again to play his shot.

Bloke: "PsSSSSSSSS."

Bert: "Yes what is it?"

Bloke: "How are you playing?"

Bert: "If you must know absolutely crap."

Bloke: "OK. Give me your card then."

MR M SPROAT (BARKINGSIDE, ESSEX)

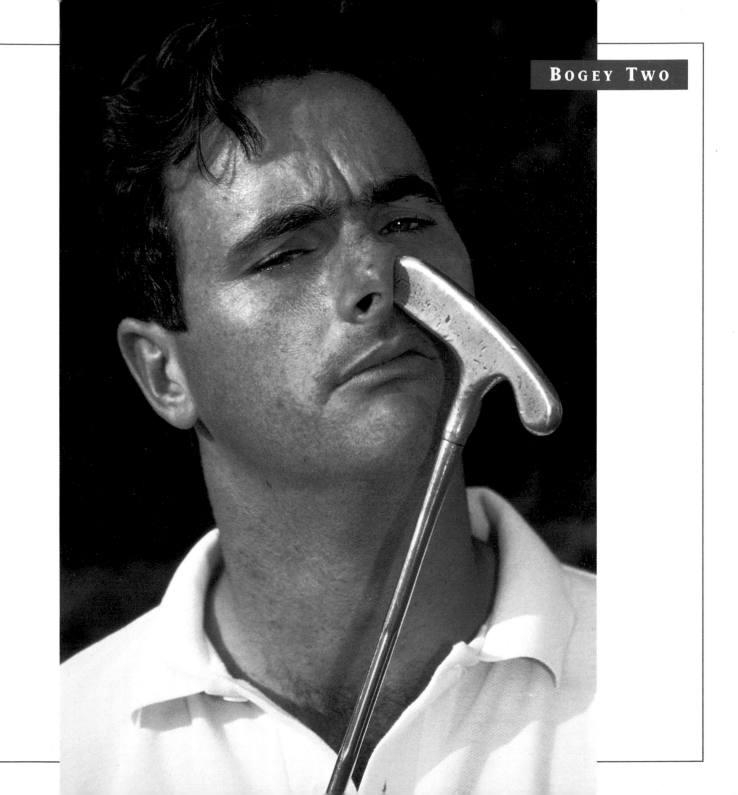

GOLF COURSES

AUGUSTA NATIONAL GOLF CLUB
AUGUSTA, GEORGIA

AT AUGUSTA THE divots tear loose on dotted lines.

JOHN UPDIKE

MUIRFIELD VILLAGE GOLF CLUB
DUBLIN, OHIO

THEY SHOULD HAVE slippers at every hole and pass a rule that you have to take off your shoes before going to the green. They shouldn't be walked on with cleats.

LEE TREVINO

PEBBLE BEACH GOLF LINKS
PEBBLE BEACH, CALIFORNIA

IF YOU'RE FIVE over par when you hit this tee, it's the best place in the world to commit suicide.

LEE TREVINO

ST ANDREWS
OLD COURSE, FIFE

I'LL TELL YOU why the Road Hole is the greatest par four in the world, it's because it's a par five!

BEN CRENSHAW

CYPRESS POINT GOLF CLUB
PEBBLE BEACH, CALIFORNIA

*QUITE SIMPLY, Cypress Point is the Sistine Chapel
of golf.*

FRANK TATUM

SPYGLASS HILL GOLF CLUB
PEBBLE BEACH, CALIFORNIA

*THEY OUGHT TO hang the man who designed this
course. Ray Charles could have done better.*

LEE TREVINO

ROYAL ST GEORGE'S
KENT

*ONE GREAT CHARACTERISTIC of Sandwich is the
extrordinary solitude that surrounds the
individual player.*

BERNARD DARWIN

THE PHOTOGRAPHERS

ALLSPORT PICTURE LIBRARY

David Cannon: pages 10, 29, 37, 43, 44, 52, 57, 58,59, 63, 66, 67, 72, 73, 75, 93, 96, 108-111, 88, 89
J. D. Cuban: pages 19, 21, 25, 57, 61, 66, 79, 82, 84, 89, 101
David Munday: pages 23, 24, 25, 55, 81, 87, 88
Stephen Dunn: pages 83, 98, 99
Gary Newkirk: pages 73, 85, 105
Richard Saker: pages 28, 74, 103
Graham Chadwick: pages 90, 91
Chris Cole: pages 48, 49
Phil Cole: pages 47, 69
Joe Mann: pages 6,7
Simon Bruty: page 57
Mike Cooper: page 55
Phil Inglis: page 41
Tim Matthews: page 60
Andrew Redington: page 39
Rick Stewart: page 57

PHIL SHELDON GOLF PICTURE LIBRARY:

pages 17, 25, 27, 35, 51, 70, 76, 94, 95, 107

ACTION PLUS

Steve Bardens: page 15
Chris Barry: page 13
Mike Hewitt: pages 31, 65

GOLF PHOTOGRAPHY INTERNATIONAL:

pages 32, 33

MATHEW HARRIS:

pages 9, 29

COVER PHOTOGRAPH:

David Cannon/Allsport